S. C. Burdett is a respected historian, linguist and theologian. She uses her knowledge to provide a distinctive understanding of the sociological, spiritual and cultural norms of bygone times and the perspectives of the people who lived in them.

To Doug, Norah and Chris Burdett.

S. C. Burdett

LIVING IN THE SPIRIT

THE LIFE AND WORK OF FIVE EARLY-MODERN VISIONARIES

AUSTIN MACAULEY PUBLISHERS™

LONDON • CAMBRIDGE • NEW YORK • SHARJAH

Austin Macauley is committed to publishing works of quality and integrity. In that spirit, we are proud to offer this book to our readers; however, the story, the experiences, and the words are the author's alone.

A CIP catalogue record for this title is available from the British Library.

ISBN 9781528981538 (Paperback)
ISBN 9781528981545 (ePub e-book)

www.austinmacauley.com

First Published (2020)
Austin Macauley Publishers Ltd
25 Canada Square
Canary Wharf
London
E14 5LQ

I would like to thank Professor Chris Durston for his tremendous support, scholarship and understanding; Professor Sue Doran and Dr Maria Dowling for their insights into this period of history; and Professor Mary Mills for sharing her knowledge of the Bible text, biblical Hebrew and New Testament Greek. I should also like to thank Professor Alec Ryrie for his continuing encouragement through the publication process. Finally, Doug, Norah and Chris Burdett and the rest of my family and friends have made this book possible by supporting me in my life-long love of learning.

Contents

.

Preface

This is a comparative study of the life, work and writings of Teresa of Avila, John of the Cross, Mary Ward, Gerrard Winstanley and George Fox, based in the first place on a detailed examination of their writings. An analysis will be made of what they shared, despite their different contexts, and where they differed. English Bible references are from the Authorised Version in preference to the Geneva Bible as Gerrard Winstanley and George Fox spent their formative years as members of the Church of England.

Chapter 1
The Biblical Narrative as
Personal Discourse

The writings of the early modern visionaries demonstrate immersion in the whole Bible text. These individuals chose as their personal discourse an experienced, internalised and owned biblical dynamic instead of the popular discourse of externalised social ritual and formal religion; their predecessors in the social milieu included Luther, Erasmus, John Fisher, Calvin and Ignatius Loyola.[1] This radical and intensely focussed approach to the Scriptures produced a reforming zeal directed towards ecclesiastical and political structures. It was in itself an outcome of the humanist and evangelical principles of Bible study and personal religious experience, which flourished first in Catholic and then in Protestant circles in the early sixteenth century. In *The Restoration of the Gospel* of 1522 Jacques Lefevre d'Etaples wrote:

> O you whom God has truly loved... know that only those are Christians who love our Lord Jesus Christ and His Word with perfect purity... for the Word of Christ

---

[1] Alister McGrath says of Erasmus: 'his characteristically humanist emphasis upon inner religion leads him to suggest that reading of Scripture *transforms* its readers, giving them a new motivation to love God and their neighbours'. *Christian theology: an introduction* (Oxford, 1994), p. 47.

is the Word of God, the Gospel of peace, liberty, and joy, the Gospel of salvation, redemption, and life.[2]

The aristocratic Argula von Grumbach, writing in protest to the University of Ingolstadt in 1522 for their arrest of Arastius Seehoffer for his Lutheran views, argued solely from precisely such an internalised and emotionally rooted experience of scriptural texts:

> ah, but what a joy it is when the spirit of God teaches us and gives us understanding flitting from one text to the next – God be praised – so that I came to see the true, genuine light shining out... if the Lord gives me grace... I don't find such promises from human beings, or papal laws or utterances.[3]

Access to the Bible came in different forms for Catholic and Protestant visionaries. For members of religious communities, exposure to the text was primarily through immersion in the Latin of the Divine Office and the Mass. Protestants, on the other hand, attended Sunday and mid-week meetings based on biblical texts in their own language and were obliged by their own religious protocol to read the Bible for themselves in the vernacular. English Protestants heard Cranmer's Prayer book in formal observance and would read translations such as Tyndale, the text and commentaries of the 1599 Geneva Bible or the King James Bible independently, with their family or with friends. The Geneva Bible also came in a pocket edition so that people 'could study it in the privacy of their homes, or could produce it in a church or an alehouse to knock down an argument with a text'.[4]

---

[2] Jacques Lefevre d'Etaples, 'The restoration of the Gospel', in *The portable Renaissance reader,* J.B. Ross and M.M. McLaughlin, eds (Harmondsworth, 1954), p. 84.
[3] Argula von Grumbach, 'To the University of Ingolstadt', in *Radical Christian writings: a reader,* A. Bradstock and C. Rowland, eds (Oxford, 2002), pp. 72-73.
[4] Hill, C., *The world turned upside-down* (London, 1991), p. 93.

In common with virtually all their contemporaries, these visionaries assented to the biblical requirement to submit themselves to their own ecclesiastical or religious authorities, following directives such as that of Paul in Romans 13:1:

> everyone must submit himself to the governing authorities, for there is no authority except that which God has established... consequently, he who rebels against the authority is rebelling against what God has instituted, and those who do so will bring judgement on themselves.

Teresa of Avila's *Life* was written only at the request of her spiritual director, and in precisely the way she was instructed, as she says in her introduction:

> the life of the holy mother Teresa of Jesus and some of the favours granted to her by God, written by herself at the command of her confessor, to whom she submits and directs it... having been commanded... to describe my way of prayer and the favours which the Lord has granted me, I wish that I had been allowed to describe also... my grave sins... but I may not do so. In fact, I have been put under severe restrictions... I pray Him with all my heart for the grace to write this account that my confessor demands of me.[5]

John of the Cross stated this principle equally assertively throughout his mystical writings, as in the *Ascent of Mount Carmel*:

> it is not my intention to depart from the sound sense and doctrine of our Holy Mother the Catholic Church; for in such a case I submit and resign myself wholly,

---

[5] Teresa of Avila, *The life of Saint Teresa,* J.M. Cohen, trans. and ed. (Harmondsworth, 1958), p. 21.

not only to her command, but to whatever better judgement she may pronounce concerning it.[6]

Later on in the work he added:

we must be guided in all these things by the law of Christ made man, and by that of His Church, and of His ministers... so much so that Saint Paul says these words: *Quod si Angelus de coelo evangelizaverit, praeterquam quod evangelizavimus vobis, anathema sit.*[7]

Likewise, Mary Ward strove diligently to do what the hierarchy requested. Having received her vision of a just soul, she wrote to her Jesuit confessor and spiritual director Fr Roger Lee,

I would exceedingly gladly, both for my better satisfaction and greater security, acquaint you with what has occurred in these two days... I... dare not embrace it for truly good till it be approved.[8]

She clearly instructed her nuns to be equally submissive: 'our sisters will never live contentedly, if they do not diligently endeavour to have but one will and one intention with their superior'.[9] Gerrard Winstanley did not engage in political activity unilaterally or in defiance of authority; instead, he consistently acknowledged the validity of the government and magistrates by actively seeking persuasive

---

[6] John of the Cross, *Ascent of Mt Carmel,* E. Allison Peers, trans. and ed. (Wheathampstead, 1974), p. 11.

[7] Ibid., p. 165, quoting Galatians 1:8: 'If any angel from Heaven preach any gospel unto you than that which we have preached unto you, let him be accursed and excommunicated'.

[8] Ward, M., in *The heart and mind of Mary Ward,* IBVM, ed. (Wheathampstead, 1985), p. 18.

[9] Ibid, p. 69.

dialogue with them, rather than rejecting social order as did the Ranters. Thus Winstanley and his fellow Diggers wrote in their *Appeal to the House of Commons*: 'the cause of this our presentment before you is an appeal to you… we… have been ever friends to the Parliament'.[10] This disposition was clearly illustrated in his opening and conclusion to *The Law of Freedom in a Platform*. It was 'humbly presented to Oliver Cromwell, General of the Commonwealth's Army in England, Scotland and Ireland', and ends 'I leave this in your hand, humbly prostrating myself and it before you'.[11] At the beginning of his career, George Fox demonstrated the same attitude in his strenuous attempts to seek advice on his spiritual condition of 'despair and temptations' from a variety of 'priests', including Nathaniel Stephens, the 'ancient priest at Mancetter in Warwickshire', 'a priest living about Tamworth', 'one called Dr Craddock, of Coventry' and 'one Macham, a priest in high account'.[12]

Requirements of church hierarchy and state, however, were not always consistent with the biblical texts and the inner promptings of the Spirit. On such occasions, early modern visionaries felt they had no choice but to prioritise their accountability to God, as this was the case in Scriptural narratives such as the accounts of Paul.[13] This in turn evoked opposition and so far from indulging in a life of unquestioning conformity, the visionaries found themselves subjected to the emotional trauma and physical dangers of rejection, hostility and even imprisonment by the very authorities with whom they were seeking to comply. George Fox rapidly found

---

[10] Winstanley, John Barker, and Thomas Star, *An appeal to the House of Commons*, in *'The Law of Freedom' and other writings,* C. Hill, ed. (Cambridge, 1983), p. 111.

[11] Winstanley, *The Law of Freedom in a Platform*, in ibid., p. 273-5.

[12] Fox, *The Journal of George Fox,* N. Penney, ed. (London, 1944), pp. 4-5.

[13] Paul was arrested, imprisoned and executed for his refusal to cease preaching the Gospel: Acts 22-28, Philippians 1:13.

himself unable to accept the 'priests' and their 'steeple-houses' as he immersed himself in the Bible and prayer and felt led by God to reject organised religion:

> my relations were much troubled that I would not go with them to hear the priest; for I would get into the orchard, or the fields, with my Bible by myself. I asked them, "Did not the apostle say to believers, that they needed no man to teach them, but as the anointing teacheth them?"[14]

This persistent and uncompromising focus on obeying God, guided by the prompting of the Spirit, resulted in recurrent antagonism from authority and imprisonment for Fox and other early modern Quakers. Winstanley encountered hostility from landlords, the magistrates of Kingston Court and subsequently the army as 'within a little time I was made obedient to the word in that particular likewise; for I took my spade and went and broke the ground upon George Hill in Surrey'.[15] As Mary Ward sought to obey God as a pioneer of government by a female General Superior and non-enclosure, she 'had many enemies' and was imprisoned at the Poor Clare convent at the Anger, Munich, in 1631.[16] Teresa faced opposition from her provincial but pressed on with her new foundation of the reformed convent of St Joseph's as prayer and visions convinced her this was from God,[17] and John of the Cross endured imprisonment, floggings, solitary confinement and near-starvation by the Calced Carmelites in Avila and Toledo from December 1577 to August 1578 for obeying what he believed were God's demands to reform his order.[18]

---

[14] Fox, *Journal,* p. 7.

[15] Winstanley, *A Watch-Word to The City of London, and the Army*, p. 128.

[16] Ward, *The heart and mind of Mary Ward,* p. 13.

[17] Teresa, *Life,* p. 238.

[18] Brenan, G., *St John of the Cross: his life and poetry* (Cambridge, 1995), pp. 28-35.

Having got themselves into such apparently contradictory, painful and insoluble situations, early-modern visionaries did not become locked into resentment, disillusion or manipulation. Instead, they demonstrated an impressive consistency of determination by resolutely applying biblical principles of non-violence and trust in God, explicitly stated in texts such as 'love your enemies, do good to them which hate you, bless them that curse you, and pray for them which despitefully use you. And unto him that smiteth thee on the one cheek offer also the other',[19] and 'trust in the Lord with all thine heart; and lean not unto thine own understanding. In all thy ways acknowledge him, and he shall direct thy paths'.[20] Teresa followed all these instructions as her plans for the new convent of St Joseph met with hostility; amidst the 'gossip at my expense... I... saw quite well that in many respects my opponents were right... I was therefore silent... I was quite content and happy'.[21] She persevered, and in the end she got exactly what she wanted. John of the Cross did not abandon his principles but was gracious and patient towards the Calced monks who imprisoned him.[22] Upon her imprisonment, Mary Ward simply continued to apply the principle of obedience until the Pope ordered her release.[23] George Fox did not give ground on his principles but neither did he retaliate. In Cambridge in 1655 he felt himself to be in such danger of violence from 'these rude scholars' because 'they knew I was so against the trade of preaching' that he was fetched by the mayor Samuel Spalding and protected in his house, where the Friends held a good meeting 'in the power of God'. The next day, following Jesus' example of slipping away from enemies, Fox escaped safely by leaving early: 'our passing away early in the morning frustrated their evil purposes against us... the Lord's power carried us through many snares

---

[19] Luke 6:27-29.
[20] Proverbs 3:5-6.
[21] Teresa, *Life,* p. 241.
[22] Brenan, *St John of the Cross,* p. 31.
[23] Ward, *The heart and mind of Mary Ward,* p. 13.

and dangers'.[24] Winstanley wrote in *A New-year's Gift for the Parliament and Army* that,

> the lords of manors have sent to beat us, to pull down our houses, spoil our labours; yet we are patient, and never offered any violence to them again, this 40 weeks past, but wait upon God with love till their hearts thereby be softened.[25]

This courageous and unlikely response to adversity may be understood easily when the Bible is seen as personal discourse. While it is true that the visionaries were still circumscribed in practical terms by their cultural milieu, they chose to undergo a transformation of their affective and intellectual inner structure precisely as described in the Scripture. Following this fundamental re-positioning of the character, their self-perception was no longer controlled and defined primarily by outside factors such as ecclesiastical norms, role in the social hierarchy, education, personal history and gender but instead by identification with the character of Christ brought about by the action of the Spirit within. Paul wrote of this specifically in his letter to the Galatians; 'you are all the children of God by faith in Christ Jesus... there is neither Jew nor Greek, there is neither bond nor free, there is neither male nor female: for ye are all one in Christ Jesus'.[26] The visionaries took as spiritual truths to be internalised, lived and experienced the biblical teachings on being born again in the Spirit, becoming children of God the Father, dying to one's old psyche, being transformed into the likeness of Christ, being filled with the Spirit and so becoming the temple of the indwelling Spirit of God. These teachings supplanted the discourses of the contemporary cultural milieu to become reality in the personal discourse of the visionaries. They accepted the scriptural teaching that a dual process of rebirth

---

[24] Fox, *Journal,* pp. 111-112.

[25] Winstanley, *A New-year's Gift for the Parliament and Army,* p. 174.

[26] Galatians 3:26, 28.

and sanctification took place through the action of the Holy Spirit. For the visionaries, as the cross of suffering was embraced the darker self was confronted and its inner crucifixion occurred. Hence all opposition, Satanic or human, became constructive in personal growth, following the example of Jesus: 'Jesus the author and finisher of our faith; who for the joy that was set before him endured the cross, despising its shame, and is set down at the right hand of the throne of God'.[27] The outcome was a psychological and affective resurrection which for them resulted in inner freedom, radical moral regeneration and integration of the personality – spiritual, emotional and intellectual. John of the Cross explained this process as follows:

> as Saint John himself says… *Nisi quis renatus fuerit ex aqua, et Spiritu Sancto, non potest videre regnum Dei.* This signifies: he that is not born again in the Holy Spirit will not be able to see this kingdom of God, which is the state of perfection; and to be born again in the Holy Spirit in this life is to have a soul most like to God in purity, having in itself no admixture of imperfection, so that pure transformation can be wrought in it through participation of union.[28]

Winstanley and Teresa described in particularly vivid terms how trials and difficulties (that is, the cross) are the means of bringing this transformation to fulfilment. Winstanley did not see his personal struggle in terms of human allies and enemies, but as a part of the cosmic conflict manifested in all history and in all individuals. The 'two-fold kingly power' was a core concept throughout his writing:

> the one is the kingly power of righteousness, and this is the power of Almighty God, ruling the whole creation in peace and keeping it together. And this is the power of universal love, leading people unto all truth…

---

[27] Hebrews 12:2.
[28] John of the Cross, *Ascent of Mt. Carmel,* p. 77.

striving with flesh and blood… this is indeed Christ himself, who will cast out the curse… but the other kingly power is the power of unrighteousness, which indeed is the devil.[29]

How this struggle is won is described with remarkable passion in *Fire in the Bush*. It has three stages: the first is of innocent 'plain-heartedness', the second one of corrupt bondage to 'imaginary powers' or evil and the third is of freedom in Christ. Winstanley is describing a universal condition from which there is no opt-out—'every branch of mankind is under one of these three estates: first either in his innocence, or secondly under the power of the curse, or thirdly under grace, or the power of the blessing'.[30] The second stage involves intense inner pain for the individual as

> this light strives against darkness in him. He sees pride striving against humility, envy against love, contentedness against anger, uncleanness of flesh against chastity, sorrow against comfort, and so cries out, *oh wretched man that I am, who shall deliver me from this body of death* or bondage to which I am a slave?… this is the time of the battle within thee… this dividing of time is the sharpest and hottest time.[31]

The final victory is achieved through Christ –

> and now one step further… and then the man enters into rest. And this is when the seed of blessing in thee kills that serpent and casts him out, and takes possession of thee and rules in righteousness in thee. For now all enemies are subdued under the anointing's feet, and he

---

[29] Winstanley, *A New-year's Gift for the Parliament and Army*, p. 162.
[30] Winstanley, *Fire in the Bush*, pp. 248-257.
[31] Ibid., p. 260.

now delivers up the kingdom to his Father... in whom there is no sorrow. [32]

Ultimately difficulties were accepted as friends in disguise by the visionaries on their path to self-realisation as biblical Christians. When the pain of enemy or friendly fire followed obeying the inner voice, it was utilised to achieve a deeper level of experience of God as every attack by Satanic powers resulted in an extension of the kingdom of God within. Therefore the visionaries did not need to fear the consequences of obedience or become enmeshed in disabling and destructive attitudes of hatred or antagonism towards anyone as it was not the person's fault, it was Satan's, and God would resolve it.[33] Teresa described this in her response to the opposition she faced against founding St Joseph's and her feelings of rejection and betrayal by those closest to her:

> I was very unpopular throughout the convent for wanting to found a more strictly enclosed house... what greatly distressed me was that my confessor wrote to me... as if I had been acting against his instructions... I became quite upset and plunged into the deepest affliction. But the Lord, who never failed me... often consoled and strengthened me... the Lord now showed me what a mighty blessing it is to suffer trials and persecutions for Him. I saw such a growth of love for God in my soul and other graces as well, that I was quite astonished and could not cease to desire even more trials.[34]

---

[32] Ibid., p. 260.

[33] Ephesians 6:12, 17-18: 'for we wrestle not against flesh and blood, but against principalities, against powers, against the rulers of the darkness of this world, against spiritual wickedness in high places. And take the helmet of salvation, and the sword of the Spirit, which is the word of God; praying always with all prayer and supplication in the Spirit'.

[34] Teresa, *Life,* pp. 241-242.

John of the Cross was 'carried away in ecstasy' when enduring the appalling conditions of imprisonment and told the nun Ana de San Alberto that 'one single grace of those that God gave me there could not be paid for by many years of prison'.[35]

Furthermore, the relationship of the believer to God as a son whose inner being had been transformed into a filial likeness had profound implications for the relationship of the individual with the divine; the love, intimacy and trust which this imparted led to empowerment and assurance as the visionary moved in the certainty of being God's agent, and gave a guarantee of being the immediate recipient of God's personal loving and gracious directions. Mary Ward wrote of the Just Soul, 'this state leads to inherited justice and conforms to Christ our Lord'.[36] The visionaries felt themselves to be actually 'rooted and grounded in love', as they were anointed with the Spirit within and experienced the overwhelming love of God and intimate joining with him. John of the Cross stated that the entire aim of the contemplative life is 'union with the Beloved... to attain to the Divine light of the perfect union of the love of God... the sweetest touches and unions'.[37] Mary Ward wrote, 'there is no love I desire or esteem like to His... be not content only to love God, but strive to be wholly lost in His love'.[38] Fox explained his inner condition thus:

> now was I come up in spirit through the flaming sword, into the paradise of God. All things were new; and all the creation gave another smell unto me than before, beyond what words can utter. I knew nothing but pureness, and innocency, and righteousness, being renewed up into the image of God by Christ Jesus.[39]

---

[35] Brenan, *St John of the Cross,* pp. 32-33.

[36] Ward, *The heart and mind of Mary Ward,* p. 20.

[37] John of the Cross, *Ascent of Mt Carmel,* pp. 10-11, 177.

[38] Ward, *The heart and mind of Mary Ward,* pp. 41, 54.

[39] Fox, *Journal,* p. 17.

Winstanley described how

> the innocence, light and purity of mankind is this, when
> the spirit of universal love lives in him and he lives in
> love, enjoying the sweet union and communion of
> spirit… Jesus Christ… is that powerful spirit of love.40

As a natural outcome of this filial relationship of love and
dependency, virtuous actions were based not on imposed
religious obligation, neither were they magical or mechanistic
attempts to earn salvation. Instead, godly behaviour was a free
and abundant expression of the Spirit, just as described by
Paul and James; 'the fruit of the Spirit is love, joy, peace,
longsuffering, gentleness, goodness, faith, meekness,
temperance:[41] I will shew you my faith by my works'.[42] John
of the Cross wrote how 'the soul… is transformed in God
through love… nothing will then remain in it that is not the
will of God'.[43] Mary Ward described her Just Soul in such
terms; 'the felicity of this course… was a singular freedom…
with an entire application and apt disposition to all good
works',[44] and warned, 'do not let the foolish world persuade
you that virtue is difficult, for the Eternal Truth says, 'My
yoke is easy and my burden light'.[45] Teresa described the
radical contrast between the grace of God and the struggle to
attain virtue herself:

> blessed be God for ever, for giving me in one moment
> the freedom that I had been unable to attain for myself,
> despite all my efforts during so many years… as this

---

[40] Winstanley, *A New-year's Gift to Parliament and the Army,* pp. 189, 204.
[41] Galatians 5:22.
[42] James 2:18.
[43] John of the Cross, *Ascent of Mt Carmel,* p. 76.
[44] Ward, *The heart and mind of Mary Ward,* p. 19.
[45] Ibid., p. 59.

was the work of One who is almighty and the true Lord of all, it gave me no pain at all.[46]

Fox contrasted his miserable state when he first attempted 'to rely wholly on the Lord alone... I cannot declare the misery I was in, it was so great and heavy upon me', with the release he experienced when God intervened:

> one day when I had been walking solitarily... I was taken up in the love of God... it was opened unto me by the eternal light and power, and I saw clearly therein that all was done, and to be done, in and by Christ; and how He conquers and destroys this tempter, the Devil, and all his works, and is atop of him; and that all these troubles were good for me, and temptations for the trial of my faith, which Christ had given me.[47]

Winstanley elaborated in detail how 'Jesus Christ... had not an imaginary covetous power in him... the power of darkness... which is the devouring dragon, had no place... in him; for the dragon was cast out'. The individual experienced the same process:

> when the power of lust is killed within, by the blessing or the seed rising up, then outward objects troubles not nor enslaves the man... they that are at liberty within, in whom the seed is risen to rule, do conquer all enemies by love and patience, and make use of any outward object with moderation.[48]

Above all, the initiative and continuing motivation for all this was providential and came from God by his grace, not from the individual, who responded only because enabled to do so by God. Teresa described her raptures thus:

---

[46] Teresa, *Life,* p. 173.
[47] Fox, *Journal,* pp. 8, 9.
[48] Winstanley, *Fire in the Bush,* pp. 270-271.

here there is no possibility of resisting... although this is delightful, the weakness of our nature makes us afraid at first... I used to remember St Paul's saying that he was 'crucified unto the world'... the agony carries with it so great a joy... this grace comes from the Lord.[49]

John of the Cross wrote of 'being born again through grace'.[50] Mary Ward wrote:

that hope remains still, that our Lord let me see it [the vision of the Just Soul], to invite me that way, and because He would give me grace in time to arrive to such an estate... in humble self-surrender I will wish for what His providence arranges for me.[51]

Winstanley consistently wrote of how Christ would defeat the imaginary power of the dragon in humanity – 'when Christ the anointing spirit rises up and enlightens mankind'[52] – and advised those struggling with evil within,

therefore whatsoever your condition is, murmur not at it, but wait; he that is come to others will come to you, and not tarry. His power and name is love, and he will conquer all by love and patience.[53]

Fox consistently stated in his *Journal* that every successful outcome of preaching or prayer was thanks to God's grace alone. This was given when needed, though sometimes patience was required:

---

[49] Teresa, *Life,* pp. 136-141.
[50] John of the Cross, *Ascent of Mt. Carmel,* p. 77.
[51] Ward, *The heart and mind of Mary Ward,* pp. 19,43.
[52] Winstanley, *Fire in the Bush,* p. 241.
[53] Ibid., p. 262.

during the time I was prisoner at Charing-Cross there came abundance to see me... priests, professors, officers of the army... a company of officers... desired me to pray with them. I sat still, with my mind retired to the Lord. At last I felt the power and spirit of God move in me, and the Lord's power did so shake and shatter them that they wondered.[54]

It is in this context that the visionaries' concepts of prayer, study, human relationships and action in the world must be seen. These individuals lived an interior joining with God, radical transformation of the character and an intense and profound desire to focus every thought, feeling and action on doing God's will as they followed Paul's instructions to 'pray without ceasing'.[55]

For Teresa, John of the Cross and Mary Ward this injunction included formal observance; for Winstanley the community of believers was synonymous with the prophetic community while engaged in direct action, and after this, a return to the parish church in Cobham and later involvement with the Quakers;[56] and for Fox it entailed first compliance with ecclesiastical demands, then a complete rejection of formal religion and finally the formation of a new Christian group. Whether ritual was accepted or not, inner personal dialogue with God was the priority; Catholic visionaries used formal outward observance as a vehicle for this internal relationship, but when Protestant visionaries found it impeded their connection with God, they rejected it.

Attitudes to academic study of the Bible were also fundamentally similar, but expressed in different forms. For all the visionaries, the aim was to own the Bible message under the direction of God by the Spirit within; 'teach me to

---

[54] Fox, *Journal,* pp. 106-107.
[55] 1 Thessalonians 5:17.
[56] Alsop, J., 'Gerrard Winstanley: what do we know of his life?' in *Winstanley and the Diggers 1649-1999,* A. Bradstock, ed. (London, 2000), p. 30.

do thy will; for thou art my God: thy spirit is good; lead me into the land of uprightness'.[57] Learning was not the path to understanding God, as wisdom could come only by the Spirit giving revelation through the Word. Teresa and John of the Cross respected academic learning, seeing it as a means to support this understanding, whereas by contrast Winstanley and Fox perceived the efforts of the university-trained theologians and philosophers as being antagonistic to a true grasp of Scripture. What all the visionaries shared was a perception that intellectual understanding must be initiated and led by the Spirit, not by theological or philosophical systems.

Supernatural manifestations were placed in precisely the same context. They were not seen as intrinsically good or bad but had value only insofar as they served to strengthen the connection between the individual and God. If they were considered to be consistent with Biblical imperatives and the leading of the Spirit, they were vital expressions of divine power; if not, they were the work of Satan and to be avoided. Teresa and John in particular advised great caution in this area, in line with Jesus' warning that miraculous powers were worse than useless when they were not clearly and specifically from God:

> not everyone that saith unto me, Lord, Lord, shall enter into the kingdom of heaven; but that doeth the will of my Father which is in heaven. Many will say to me in that day, Lord, Lord, have we not prophesied in thy name? And in thy name have cast out devils? And in the name done many wonderful works? And then will I profess unto them, I never knew you: depart from me, ye that work iniquity.[58]

---

[57] Psalm 143:10.
[58] Matthew 7:21-23.

28

The writer of Acts described how Paul used the authority of Jesus to cast out a destructive spirit:

> a certain damsel possessed with a spirit of divination met us, which brought her masters much gain by soothsaying… but Paul, being grieved, turned and said to the spirit, 'I command thee in the name of Jesus Christ to come out of her'. And he came out the same hour.[59]

There was a wide range of charismatic expressions of the Spirit; every individual expressed more than one, though not necessarily all. Elijah prophesied, saw visions, heard the voice of God and worked miracles, as did Jesus and the apostles, not as ends in themselves but to enlarge the kingdom of God on earth. The early modern visionaries experienced signs and wonders for the same reason as they sought to be filled with the same spirit.

This focus on restructuring the inner self in conformity with Biblical models resulted in close affective bonds with like-minded individuals engaged in the same process, in line with biblical commands to love one another but overriding usual considerations of social bonding according to gender or social rank. Teresa and John wrote of the intense love they felt for their co-religionists, male and female, secular or in community. Mary Ward wrote of her attachment to her sister nuns and Winstanley of his love for his fellow Diggers. Fox and the Friends wrote in intensely emotional terms of their profound sense of connection with and love for each other. As might be expected, the visionaries took great care to express their affections in godly and biblical ways, scorning any improper or abusive behaviour and showing respect and kindness towards each other.

The outcome of such dedication to the leading of the Spirit and modelling themselves on the Bible narrative was in every case prophetic. The purpose of prophetic action in the Bible was always to bring about God's kingdom of justice and peace

---

[59] Acts 16:16-18.

on earth within the individual and within society. The prophets preached repentance so that the individual could find how 'the kingdom of God is within you'[60] and engaged in direct action to bring about change in political and ecclesiastical structures. Hence Teresa's and John's detailed writings on interior prayer combined with active reforming zeal, Mary Ward's spiritual directives to her nuns went alongside the foundation and work of her order, Winstanley's ecstatic spiritual directives combined with direct political action and pamphleteering, and Fox's journal contained descriptions of intense spiritual experience together with the prophetic ministry round 'steeple-houses' and the founding of the Quakers.

It can be seen therefore that an immersion in the biblical text and a decision to embrace this text as reality led to a profound inner transformation for all the visionaries. This in turn resulted in a fundamental repositioning of their relationships with other individuals and social and ecclesiastical structures, and gave them a passionate zeal to reform and renew those around them.

---

[60] Luke 17:21.

Chapter 2
Visions and Voices

The early modern visionaries inhabited a cultural milieu in which 'astrology, divination, animism and fear of nature, alchemy, sorcery, demonic possession, witchcraft and belief in magical healing were all part of the normal outlook... accepted by the majority of the educated and illiterate alike'.[61]

Catholics had always accepted the reality of miracles and visions, such as those of Francis of Assisi and Julian of Norwich; although the word-based nature of Protestantism did not encourage manifestations of the supernatural, these were still part of everyday life in Protestant countries, and for more committed Protestants, prophecy and revelation were indispensable aspects of faith. The growing rejection of scholastic systematic theology and the acceptance of humanistic and evangelical principles amongst the intelligentsia at the beginning of the early-modern period did not challenge this world-view but provided more evidence for it, as John Walter summarises: 'broader intellectual changes, notably those historians label Neoplatonists, reinforced this vision of the world as an animistic universe full of vibrant forces which could be tapped'.[62]

Thus Jewish mystical Cabalistic teaching, originating in Spain and revealed to the Catholic Ramon Lull in a vision (1274), was taken up by humanist Christians as the Jews were

---

[61]Munck, T., *Seventeenth-century Europe: state, conflict and the social order in Europe 1598-1700* (London, 1990), p. 269.

[62] Walter, J., 'The commons and their mental worlds', in *The Oxford illustrated history of Tudor and Stuart Britain,* J. Morrill, ed. (Oxford, 2000), p. 195.

expelled from Spain in 1492 and spread across Europe.[63] Reuchlin used his Hebrew expertise to prove the Tetragrammaton was the Name of Jesus[64] and the Venetian Franciscan Francesco Giorgi (1466-1540) used the Cabala to 'support evangelical reform' as well as applying its methods to manipulate 'miraculous and magical powers'.[65] Agrippa described how 'there is a bad magic which calls on bad demons; there is a good magic which calls on angels through the Cabala'.[66] According to Frances Yates, Milton's *Il Penseroso* describes a Cabalistic 'visionary trance;' 'Milton's melancholy inspiration is also demonic, but a white ascetic magic... connecting with higher realms of prophecy and angelic hierarchies'.[67] In popular culture, wonder-working saints and shrines were approved and controlled by Church authorities in Catholic countries such as Spain, where fifty-three curing images and relics were recorded in various authorised places such as monasteries and chapels in the sixteenth century.[68] During the English Revolution, there were multiple published accounts of the miraculous; the chapbook *Strange and fearful news from Plaisto in the Parish of Westham* (1645) described the experiences of 'one Paul Fox, a silk weaver', as many thousands of people testified to the haunting of his house – a sword danced, a boulder bounced up the stairs, and Fox heard rapping at the door and a voice calling out, 'I must dwell there'.[69]

Thus the early-modern visionaries shared a culture of visions, prophecy and the supernatural with their

---

[63] Yates, F., *The occult philosophy of the Elizabethan Age* (London, 2000), p. 15.

[64] Johannes Reuchlin, '*De verbo mirifico'*, p. 192, Lyons, 1552, in Frances Yates, *The occult philosophy of the Elizabethan Age,* plate 2.

[65] Yates, *The occult philosophy of the Elizabethan Age,* pp. 40-41.

[66] Ibid., p. 49.

[67] Ibid., pp. 66-67.

[68] Christian, W.A., *Local Religion in Sixteenth-century Spain* (Guildford, 1989), p. 94.

[69] Friedman, J., *Miracles and the pulp press during the English revolution* (London, 1993), p. 23.

contemporaries. However, the visionaries' experiences differed profoundly in that their aim was to be conformed to the likeness of Jesus by submitting themselves to the will of God as revealed in Scripture by the power of the Holy Spirit within. Whether revelations, signs and wonders occurred was for them subject to the will of God and not the outcome of human desires to manipulate the environment for one's own ends, good or bad. The visionary was an agent of God as He worked from their innermost being, a dynamic more personal than even that of Old Testament visionaries such as Elijah, who had the Spirit on but not in them. Thus they did not seek to control their physical or spiritual environment through religious magic as did popular Catholicism with its relics and shrines, by manipulating angels and demons as did the Cabalists, or by controlling natural energies as did the cunning men and women.

What differentiated visionaries such as Teresa from many of their contemporaries was firstly this fixed determination to do only what they considered to be directly from God, and secondly their conviction that their power came only from God and not from any other external invisible force, benevolent or malefic. The only element of control was seen in their obedience to Jesus' instructions to take authority over malevolent demonic forces, which were on no account to be utilised but rebuked and sent packing by the believer in the power of the Spirit within; by resisting these forces the visionary developed a greater reliance on God and a deeper experience of godly spiritual power. Physical manifestations were in any case treated with extreme caution as it was generally held that they could come from Satan and all the early-modern visionaries insisted that the visions, locutions and revelations they received from God were all interior or mental. In sixteenth-century Spain, nuns, friars, *beatas* and peasants were taken before the Inquisition for false or diabolical visions, *raptos y extasis,* and Diego Perez de Valdiva warned nuns not to have visions in his *Aviso de Gente recogida y especialmente dedicada al servicio de Dios*

(1585).[70] Teresa warned her readers that 'the proof that something comes from God lies in its conformity to Holy Scripture'[71] and advised them against seeking visionary experience for its own sake; so did John of the Cross, as he taught that this leads the soul to 'fall into abominations and deceits'.[72] Similarly, Calvin had set the tone for Protestants when he valued revelation and prophecy only as enlightening understanding of the Scriptures, stating that the office of prophet 'either does not exist today or is less commonly seen'.[73] John Uitenhovius, writing to Henry Bullinger on the German congregation in London (April 9, 1551), described how 'a system of discipline is now established by us... a part of which is... the catechism... and also prophesying, or a collation of the scriptures'.[74] For members of the radical sects during the Interregnum, a wide range of supernatural manifestations were accepted, provided they were rooted in Scriptural understanding and came from the Holy Spirit within. Thus visionary experience was seen primarily a means whereby God transformed the mind and spirit into the likeness of Jesus and secondarily a way in which the power of God could more effectively be brought to others within the visionary's sphere of influence; God 'gives himself to such persons, by supernatural means, for the profit of His Church and of its members'.[75] In conformity with models found in the Scriptural narrative, a range of visionary experience could be expected, but it was always appropriate to the inner transformation of the visionary and to the needs of those around and not a fixed programme of manifestations.

---

[70] Christian, *Local religion in sixteenth-century Spain,* p. 90.

[71] Teresa of Avila, *Life,* p. 179.

[72] John of the Cross, *Ascent of Mt Carmel,* p. 285.

[73] Calvin, J., *Institutes of the Christian Religion,* J.T. McNeill, ed., and F.L. Battles, trans. (Philadelphia, 1960), p. 1057.

[74] Uitenhovius, 'John Uitenhovius to Henry Bullinger', in *Original letters relative to the English Reformation,* H. Robinson, ed. (Cambridge, 1847), p. 587.

[75] John of the Cross, *Ascent of Mt Carmel,* p. 285.

It is in this context that the spiritual experiences of all the visionaries must be understood. An analysis of the writings of Teresa of Avila, John of the Cross, Mary Ward, Gerrard Winstanley and George Fox shows close similarities in terms of motivation and spiritual intention together with a variety of expressions of charismata matched to the requirements of their missions. A distinction can be made between revelation of the will of God through the emotions, mind, spirit or supernatural means, and the prophetic action taken subsequent to these instructions. For the visionaries, this prophetic action was always charismatic in the biblical sense of being carried out in the power or gifts of the Spirit, whether it involved such apparently politically motivated tasks as the refusal to address anyone with the formal 'you' or remove one's hat to authority, or supernatural interventions such as miraculous healings. In what follows, the visionaries' revelations will be briefly summarised while the prophetic application will be considered separately in the last chapter. These revelations came in the form of mental pictures or visions; specific words, or locutions, from God, often but not always from the Bible text; and intense and clear emotional states in which the will of God was received intuitively. The only biblically acceptable context of this visionary experience was conformity to the will of God.

Thus in her *Life* Teresa combines frequent admonitions to a holy life with descriptions of her experiences together with cautions and warnings as to the spiritual pitfalls these can present. Teresa writes that she only began to experience real progress in her prayers when she 'quite lost my trust in myself and put all my confidence in God;'[76] Teresa would make an inward picture, for example, 'in which I threw myself at Christ's feet'.[77] As a result of this interior attitude of dependence and trust,

---

[76] Teresa of Avila, *Life,* p. 67.
[77] Ibid., p. 71.

there would come to me such a feeling of the presence of God as made it impossible for me to doubt that He was within me, or that I was totally engulfed in Him. This was no kind of vision; I believe it is called mystical theology.[78]

Unlike the Cabalists or cunning men and women, Teresa was not attempting to control her experiences but relentlessly reminds her reader that all authentically Christian experience is dependent solely on the will and grace of God. Progress in visionary prayer, however, also required the individual to persevere and Teresa elaborates four stages of prayer towards 'the joy of possessing this perfect love'.[79] In the early stages, 'the labour is hardest', whereas 'in the further stages of prayer the chief thing is joy'.[80] In the initial stages of contemplation, revelations are given by God so that 'in the time of a single Credo' the individual understands more than 'in many years with all our human efforts'.[81] In the second stage of prayer, the soul 'comes into touch with the supernatural' as 'grace reveals itself more clearly'.[82] The soul receives joy which 'increases the growth of the virtues',[83] but Teresa warns that God may also lead it, 'as He led me, along the path of fear'.[84] The visionary also had to be aware that supernatural experience can come from the devil, who can 'transform himself into an angel of light'.[85] These experiences can be recognised as Satanic both by their destructive results and by revelation:

---

[78] Ibid., p. 71.
[79] Ibid., p. 76.
[80] Ibid., p. 77.
[81] Ibid., p. 86.
[82] Ibid., p. 98.
[83] Ibid., p. 99.
[84] Ibid., p. 100.
[85] Ibid., p. 101, quoting 2 Cor. 11:14.

locutions that come from the devil not only lead to no good, but leave bad effects behind them. These I have experienced, though only on two or three occasions, and each time I have had an immediate warning from the Lord that they came from the devil.[86]

Teresa dealt with attacks by the devil upon her inner peace and security by reminding herself of the Lordship of God over them: 'the devils are His slaves – and of this there can be no doubt, since it is an article of faith – what harm can they do me, who am a servant of this Lord and King?' This gave her the confidence to defy them so that 'I lost all my habitual fears for good', and 'acquired an authority over them'.[87] In the third state, 'very often I was, so to speak, bewildered and intoxicated with love'.[88] In this condition the intellect and faculties are stilled. The fourth stage describes the soul in union with God:

> the soul is conscious that it is fainting almost completely away in a kind of swoon, with a very great calm and joy. Its breath and all its bodily powers progressively fail it, so that it can hardly stir its hands without great effort. Its eyes close involuntarily... he hears but does not understand... he cannot form a word.[89]

The outcome of such prayer is unions, raptures and greater joy and virtue. In a rapture, 'you see and feel this cloud, or this powerful eagle rising and bearing you up on its wings... sometimes it has affected my whole body, which has been lifted from the ground'.[90] On one occasion, this happened in

---

[86] Ibid., p.177.
[87] Ibid., 182.
[88] Ibid., p. 113.
[89] Ibid., pp. 125-126.
[90] Ibid., pp. 136-7. Cf. Isaiah 40:31: they that wait upon the Lord shall renew their strength; they shall mount up with wings as eagles.

the choir, and on another as she felt a rapture coming she 'lay on the ground and the sisters came to hold me down'.[91] These raptures lead to an intense longing for God such that 'the soul seems to be in a state of destitution'. At such times,

> the pain is so extreme... sometimes my pulse almost ceases to beat at all... my bones are all disjointed and my hands are so rigid that sometimes I cannot clasp them together. Even next day I feel a pain in my wrists and over my whole body.

Following this 'state of destitution', 'the Lord' may bring to mind Bible verses by revelatory grace and 'without any effort of mine' and the soul will then experience 'a joy of exceeding worth'.[92] These raptures may also bring miraculous healing; 'often a person who was previously very ill, and racked with severe pain, is left healthy at the end and stronger than before'.[93] The final stage of prayer is ecstasy; 'in ecstasy come true revelations great favours, and visions, all which help to humble and strengthen the soul'.[94] These visions concerned the nature of God and of heaven and hell, prophetic words and action to be taken, and the state of Teresa's own soul and of others. This included revelations of the state of the dead: a member of the order of St Dominic 'appeared to me several times since his death in very great glory, and has informed me of certain things'.[95]

John of the Cross describes only those visionary experiences which were suitable to his didactic purpose of edifying other Catholics; the outer manifestations he experienced are described by others. On April 2, 1618, the Beatas nun M. Francisca de la Madre de Dios testified that when John of the Cross was preaching to the nuns one day

---

[91] Ibid., p. 137.
[92] Ibid., pp. 139-141.
[93] Ibid., p. 143.
[94] Ibid., p. 151.
[95] Teresa, *Life,* p. 287.

'this witness observed that on two separate occasions he was rapt and lifted up from the ground'.[96] In the *Ascent of Mount Carmel,* these experiences are repeatedly placed in the context of strict warnings against seeking them; 'wherefore he that would now enquire of God, or seek any vision or revelation, would not only be acting foolishly, but would be committing an offence against God'.[97] The visions are systematically categorised. In chapters 1-22 of the *Ascent of Mount Carmel* the elementary stages of interior prayer are described, in which visions are perceived by the senses. These are full of pitfalls because 'of the hindrance and harm that may be caused by apprehensions of the understanding which proceed from that which is supernaturally presented to the outward bodily senses'.[98] The believer then advances to a stage where these are infrequent or vanish and a 'dark night' ensues of sensory and emotional deprivation of any awareness of the presence of God. This results in spiritual purification and the believer gains 'apprehensions of the understanding that come in a purely spiritual way'.[99] As the believer perseveres further 'there are four manners of apprehension which are communicated to the spirit without the aid of any bodily sense: these are visions, revelations, locutions and spiritual feelings'.[100] The visions are of 'corporeal substances' such as the 'celestial Jerusalem' in the Apocalypse and 'incorporeal' substances 'such as angels and souls'.[101] These 'are felt in the substance of the soul, with the sweetest touches and unions'.[102] Revelations

---

[96] Peers, *The complete works of Saint John of the Cross,* p. xxv.
[97] John of the Cross, *Ascent of Mt Carmel,* p. 163.
[98] Ibid., p. 96.
[99] Ibid., pp. 173-175.
[100] Ibid., pp. 95-97.
[101] Ibid., pp. 175-176.
[102] Ibid., p. 177.

properly belong to the spirit of prophecy. With respect to this, it must first be known that revelation is naught else than the discovery of some hidden truth or the manifestation of some secret or mystery.

These are of two types: a deeper understanding of God and a revelation of 'certain things which He is doing or proposes to do'.[103] Locutions are words which 'come when the spirit is recollected and absorbed very attentively in some meditation' and are 'illumination' given to the soul 'by the Holy Spirit who teaches it'.[104] Caution is advised as these may come from Satan.[105] The believer is warned to resist malevolent deceptions by trusting in God: 'the devil... deludes it [the soul] with great ease, unless it takes the precaution of resigning itself to God', with the result that 'the devil causes many to believe in vain visions and false prophecies'.[106] Revelation may also come through the feelings and the whole of Book 3 of the *Ascent* is dedicated to these.

The experiences of those who progress even further in interior prayer are described in the *Dark night of the Soul*, and occur 'when God desires to bring them to the state of union with God. And this latter night is a more obscure and dark and terrible purgation'.[107] This is necessary to progress beyond those 'raptures and trances and dislocations of the bones which always happen when the communications are not purely spiritual'.[108] As the soul 'continues to practice and acquire the virtues and become purer, wiser and more cautious' so does 'this dark night of contemplation absorb and

---

[103] Ibid., p. 181.
[104] Ibid., pp. 195-6.
[105] Ibid., p. 201.
[106] Ibid., p. 377.
[107] Ibid., p. 18.
[108] John of the Cross, *Dark night of the Soul,* p. 375.

immerse the soul in itself... the nearer the soul approaches Him, the blacker is the darkness which it feels'.[109] Finally the

> last step of this secret ladder of love causes the soul to become wholly assimilated to God, by reason of the clear and immediate vision of God which it then possesses... there is naught that is hidden from the soul.[110]

In this condition the soul 'no longer has weakness... it is itself received into the Spirit. And thus it then has everything after the manner of the Spirit'.[111] As the soul is transformed by the inner workings of the Holy Spirit, gifts are given by God to the visionary in order to bring about the Kingdom of God on earth as in Heaven:

> the fifth kind of good thing wherein the soul may rejoice, which is the supernatural... the graces whereof Saint Paul speaks[112] – namely, faith, gifts of healing, the working of miracles, prophecy, knowledge and discernment of spirits, interpretation of words and likewise the gift of tongues... the temporal benefits are the healing of infirmities, the receiving of their sight by the blind, the raising of the dead, the casting out of devils, prophesying concerning the future so that men may take heed to themselves, and other things of the kind. The spiritual and eternal benefit is that God is known and served through these good works... supernatural works and miracles... are not in themselves a means for uniting the soul with God, as charity is.[113]

---

[109] Ibid., p. 425.
[110] Ibid., pp. 440-441.
[111] Ibid., p. 339.
[112] 1 Cor. 12:9-10.
[113] John of the Cross, *Ascent of Mt Carmel,* pp. 281-282.

Mary Ward's visionary experiences must also be seen in the context of her life of submission to the Holy Spirit and dedication to prayer. Like the other visionaries, the intensity and persistence of her desire to live in, for and through the Spirit within resulted in a consciousness of union with God, a tuning-in of her emotions to the Spirit which by-passed logical processes, and raptures, ecstasies and visions. On the feast of St Gregory in 1607, while still a novice with the Flemish Poor Clares, she wrote that 'suddenly I was enkindled with a vehement desire to procure a monastery for the English of this Order'. As she prayed for further guidance she was 'favoured' with 'frequent and clear light accompanied with peace and strength of soul far more than I ever before experienced'.[114] On St Athanasius' Day 1609 she had a further revelation in her spirit, which 'seemed to me to come from God and seized me with such force, that it annihilated me completely', that she should leave the Order of St Clare and do something entirely different, which was not revealed except that 'it was something good, and was the will of God'.[115]

Raptures were also experienced, and invariably resulted from intense dedication and perseverance through difficulties. Mary Poyntz described such an occasion as happening in 1626 on Christmas Eve in the parish church through till Christmas morning in the Franciscan chapel in Feldkirch in Austria. From Midnight Mass 'she remained till about three in the morning in as great cold as I think ever was felt, but what was more sensible to her... was an inexpressible affliction of mind which endured till nine at High Mass at the Capuchin's Church'. As she prayed for the conversion of England,

[114] Littlehales, M.M., *Mary Ward: pilgrim and mystic* (Tunbridge Wells, 1998), p. 43.
[115] Peters, H., *Mary Ward: a world in contemplation,* H. Butterworth, trans. (Leominster, 1994), p. 93.

it was clearly shown to her with what infinite and compassionate love God had encompassed Charles I and longed to have him for all eternity as a co-heir of his glory; his own co-operation alone was wanting. As she saw God's love for the King, she was rapt in ecstasy.[116]

Like Teresa and John, it was in a state of union with God that Mary received her frequent locutions and visions, though her revelation was of a life 'not like that of the saints, whose holiness chiefly appears in that union with God, which maketh them out of themselves'.[117] Her purpose was not to produce didactic spiritual writings on mystical prayer but to pursue an apostolic ministry within a religious community consisting of sisters seeking to be transformed into a state of purity and total dedication to God; it was to show her the way to achieve this that she received her revelations. Her 'Gloria vision' of 1609 confirmed her personal apostolic activity in England, in 1611 she was given the foundations for her community, and the Vision of the Just Soul in 1615 was confirmation of her congregation as the Society of Jesus, as far as it was possible for women to operate in their sphere of work.[118] These three revelations contained entirely new concepts for women's Orders. In all visions she denies any outward or sensory perceptions. The 'Glory vision' was more precisely a locution. According to her own account, she was in London engaged in practical ministry, not living in community, dressed 'in the fashion of the country and the circumstances'. While meditating 'coldly' on the practicalities of arranging a dowry to enable a young woman to enter a convent, she

---

[116] Littlehales, *Mary Ward: pilgrim and mystic,* pp. 150-151.

[117] Mary Ward, *Till God will: Mary Ward through her writings,* G. Orchard, IBVM., ed. (Slough, 1985), p. 40.

[118] Peters, H., *Mary Ward: a world in contemplation,* p. 174.

had a second infused light in a manner as before, but much more distinct; that the work to be was not a monastery of Teresians, but a thing much more grateful to God and so great an augmentation of his glory as I cannot declare.

It was still not revealed to Mary exactly what this should be, except that she was not to be a Carmelite and that it was to be something entirely new, and the words 'Glory, Glory, Glory', sounded in her ears for more than two hours.[119]

Her spiritual revelation of 1611 is described in a letter she wrote to Nuntius Albergati in 1612.[120] She was alone and 'sick in great extremity' but 'in some extraordinary repose of mind' when

> I heard distinctly, not by sound of voice but intellectually understood, these words *Take the same of the Society...* these few words gave so great measure of light in that particular Institute, comfort and strength, and changed so the whole soul, as that it was impossible for me to doubt but that they came from him.[121]

In other words, Mary was being instructed by God to take the name of Jesus, as used by the Society of Jesus. The Vision of the Just Soul was given when Mary was on retreat for eight days at St Omer before the Feast of All Saints, 1615. She wrote an account of this vision to Fr Lee and it is depicted on the twenty-fifth picture of the *Painted Life,* the series of fifty pictures painted within forty years of her death recording significant events of Mary's life.[122] In it, Mary was shown the spiritual state of those who would be members of the Institute: 'it seems a certain clear and perfect estate, to be had in this

---

[119] Ibid., p. 174.

[120] Ibid., p. 115.

[121] Orchard, *Till God will: Mary Ward through her writings,* p. xxvii.

[122] Byrne, L., *Mary Ward: a pilgrim finds her way* (Dublin, 1984), p. 6.

life, and such an one is altogether needful for those that should well discharge the duties of this Institute'. Like the other visionaries, including Winstanley and Fox, Mary was convinced by such revelation that purity of spirit could be achieved by grace in this life. This purity led to a state of 'felicity' and detachment, that is, freedom from entanglement in sin, and so the individual would be liberated to lead a life of abundant good works and bring about justice on earth. She continues by stating that an aspect of this justice was avoidance of hypocrisy and counterfeit religion: 'the word *justice,* and those in former times that were called just persons, works of justice, done innocently, and that we be such as we appear, and appear such as we are'. This vision gave definition to Mary's earlier revelations that she was to found a new order: as 'my meditations further discovered the condition of this Institute, methought I better understood these particulars, one by one, practically not confusedly, than ever before I had done'. These particulars were not arrived at by logical analysis of effective administrative structure but by a revelation that each member of the Institute was to be transformed by the Spirit within into the Just Soul: her meditations

> led me severally to that first estate, as the fountain and best disposition for a soul to be in that would perform all this well, and from whence I could without labour return to them again, and discern with great clearness and solid tranquillity the excellency and convenience of them.[123]

The last vision formative for her Institute was when she was in London in 1619, meditating on the words *Et vocabis nomen ejus Jesum* (and you shall call his name Jesus).[124] The inscription on the *Painted Life* states:

---

[123] Ward, *The heart and mind of Mary Ward,* pp. 18-20.
[124] IBVM, ibid., p. 20.

God showed visibly to Mary a just soul endowed with great brilliance, giving her clearly to understand that all those who live in this Institute conformably to their vocation, will attain to a similar indescribable beauty of soul, because this state leads to inherited justice and conforms to Christ our Lord, as to a most perfect model of all virtues.[125]

The focus of Gerrard Winstanley's writings is spiritual and political reform rather than miracles of healing, exorcism or visions of the supernatural. However, the foundation of his programme is visionary, ecstatic and prophetic and based on the leading of the Spirit within. He describes his mystical trance in one of his earliest writings, *The New Law of Righteousness*, published in January 1649.[126] His political action is rooted and grounded in the continued lived dynamic of interior exaltation in the Spirit and the inner victory of the power of Christ over the power of evil. The inner struggle as 'the two powers of light and darkness, Christ and the devil, strives who shall rule in this living soul first' is a constant refrain in Winstanley's writing and is specifically described in great detail in *Fire in the Bush*. As a result of the triumph of Christ in the individual, the 'third estate' is achieved,

> drawing mankind into union with the Father, making all things new and so making peace', and 'he rises up in power and glory, and makes man one with himself, and *sets* him down in rest, never to fall again.[127]

In *A Watch-word to the City of London* Winstanley describes how, after being fined at Kingston Court and having his cattle and goods taken by the bailiffs, he was 'quiet in my

---

[125] Orchard, *Till God will: Mary Ward through her writings,* p. xxviii.

[126] Aylmer, G., 'The Diggers in their own time', in *Winstanley and the Diggers 1649-1999,* A. Bradstock, ed. (London, 2000), p. 9.

[127] Winstanley, *Fire in the Bush*', p. 257.

heart and filled with comfort within myself, that the King of righteousness would cause this to work for the advancing of his own cause', and 'saying likewise in my heart as I was walking along, 'O thou King of righteousness, shew thy power', he was comforted as 'the answer in my heart was satisfactory and full of sweet joy and peace'.[128] Describing the destruction of the Diggers' houses by the soldiers, Winstanley says 'yet the diggers were mighty cheerful, and their spirits resolve to wait upon God, to see what he will do', and they rebuilt 'some few little hutches like calf-cribs, and there they lie a-nights, and follow their work a-days still with wonderful joy of heart, taking the a-spoiling of their goods cheerfully'.[129] In *Fire in the Bush,* he writes how the spirit-filled heart 'is a land of righteousness, full of life, light and fruit of peace and truth'.[130]

This inner life of dedication and peace gave an ability to hear the Spirit within and for Winstanley this was always connected with political vision. In the introduction to *A Watch-word to the City of London*, he writes of the revelation which prompted him; 'being quiet at my work, my heart was filled with sweet thoughts, and many things were revealed to me which I never read in books, nor heard from the mouth of any flesh'. He goes on to say that

> amongst those revelations this was one: that the earth shall be made a common treasury of livelihood to all mankind, without respect of person; and I had a voice within me bade me declare it all abroad, which I did obey.

---

[128] Winstanley, *A Watch-word to the City of London, and the Army,* pp. 138-140.
[129] Winstanley, *A New-year's Gift for the Parliament and Army*, p. 179.
[130] Winstanley, *Fire in the Bush*, p. 223.

The fulfilment of this word was direct action;

> within a little time I was made obedient to the word in that particular likewise; for I took my spade and went and broke the ground upon George hill in Surrey, thereby declaring freedom to the creation.[131]

The introduction to *Fire in the Bush* has a similar description: 'this following declaration of the word of life was a free gift to me from the Father himself; and I received it not from men'. Winstanley put his 'free gift' aside for 'almost a fortnight', and 'then one night as I waked out of sleep the voice was in my very heart and mouth, ready to come forth: 'Go send it to the churches'.[132] *The Law of Freedom in a Platform* was also published in obedience to the word within. It was written two years prior to its publication and put aside, 'with a thought never to bring it to light'. However,

> this word was like fire in my bones ever and anon, *Thou shalt not bury thy talent in the earth*; therefore I was stirred up to give it a resurrection, and to pick up as many of my scattered papers as I could find, and to compile them into this method, which I do here present to you, and do quiet my own spirit.[133]

Winstanley notes here how he only had peace of mind when he obeyed the directives of the Spirit within. These directives were a prophetic vision of a restructured society; Winstanley did not develop a political theory based on Plato or other analytical philosophers but instead sought to bring a Bible-based inner creative vision into reality. Thus Winstanley's ideal of equitable shared land-ownership was not the logical outcome of economic principles but came from a profound ecstatic biblical belief. Ownership of property was

---

[131] Winstanley, *A Watch-word to the City of London, and the Army*, pp. 127-128.
[132] Winstanley, *Fire in the Bush*, p. 213.
[133] Winstanley, *The Law of Freedom,* p. 285.

covetousness, part of the rule of 'the kingly power of darkness', but 'Christ is rising who will take the dominion and kingdom out of his hand'. As he writes to Parliament and the Army,

> for if this kingly power of covetousness, which is the unrighteous divider, did not yet rule, both Parliament, Army and rich people would cheerfully give consent that those we call poor should dig and freely plant the waste and common land for a livelihood (seeing there is land enough, and more by half than is made use of), and not be suffered to perish for want. And yet O ye rulers of England, you make a blazing profession that you know and that you own God, Christ and the Scriptures: but did Christ ever declare such hardness of heart? Did not he bid the rich man go and sell all that he hath and give to the poor?

This is combined with prophetic directives reminiscent of Isaiah, Hosea and Jeremiah:

> therefore you lords of manors, and you rulers of England, if you own God, Christ and Scripture, now make restitution and deliver us quiet possession of our land, which the kingly power as yet holds from us.[134]

Like the Catholic visionaries, Winstanley was aware of the Biblical teaching and experienced spiritual reality of Satanic deception and warned his readers to protect themselves against such attacks by determined resistance in prayer:

> the deceptions which the devil can bring about, and does bring about, concerning this kind of knowledge and understanding... are very great and difficult to unmask... for suggestion has sometimes great power

---

[134] Winstanley, *A New-year's Gift for the Parliament and Army*, pp. 164-165.

over the soul... causing the knowledge which it conveys to sink into the soul with such great power, persuasiveness and determination that the soul needs to give itself earnestly to prayer and to exert great strength if it is to cast it off.[135]

Such deception can be recognised by its fruit. As evil comes to the soul from the devil, he taints it with 'pride, avarice, wrath, envy, etc., and can cause it unjust hatred, or vain love, and deceive it in many ways'.[136]

George Fox's accounts in his *Journal* and reports in the *Book of Miracles* give evidence of a comprehensive range of charismatic experience. This however is not presented systematically as in Teresa's *Life* and the works of John of the Cross as Fox's didactic purpose is different. He, like Teresa in the *Book of the Foundations* and Winstanley, is recounting visionary experience embedded in and expressed through the life of the believer; his descriptions of union with the Spirit are of necessity repetitive as he acknowledges the leading of the Spirit for every single action, reinforcing the biblical teaching that 'whatsoever is not of faith is sin'.[137] These experiences were all rooted in the repeated immersion in the overwhelming love of God: 'One day when I had been walking solitarily abroad, and was come home, I was taken up in the love of God, so that I could not but admire the greatness of His love'. For Fox, as for the other visionaries, revelation was given in this state together with a profound assurance of Christ's victory over the opposing force of Satan; he continues,

> while I was in that condition it was opened unto me by the eternal light and power, and I saw clearly therein that all was done, and to be done, in and by Christ; and

---

[135] Winstanley, A *New-year's Gift for the Parliament and Army,* p. 189.
[136] Winstanley, *Fire in the Bush,* p. 222.
[137] Romans 14:23.

how He conquers and destroys this tempter, the Devil, and all his works, and is atop of him.[138]

Fox describes precisely the same process as the other visionaries; the victory over the works of Satan takes place within the believer as hardship, persecution, fear and deception are experienced and overcome by the love of Christ. This inner victory is then exercised outwardly, both in ordinary ways and in supernatural forms such as healing, discernment of spirits or exorcism, in order to bring about God's Kingdom in the world.

It was in this condition of renewal, ecstatic revelation and conformity to God's likeness that Fox exercised charismatic gifts and persevered in the face of persistent hostility, as did those in the Biblical narrative and the other early-modern visionaries. Thus Fox describes how he challenged a priest in a steeple-house who was attempting to silence a woman asking a question as he was 'wrapped up, as in a rapture, in the Lord's power'.[139] This rapturous state could also include a direct word or locution from God, as it could for Teresa, John or Mary Ward:

> I heard of a people that were in prison in Coventry for religion. And as I walked towards the jail, the word of the Lord came to me, saying, "My love was always to thee, and thou art in my love". And I was ravished with the sense of the love of God, and greatly strengthened in my inward man.

This rapturous state was immediately followed by an encounter with Satanic darkness, which Fox countered by focussing on the Spirit: 'But when I came into the jail where the prisoners were, a great power of darkness struck at me, and I sate still having my spirit gathered into the love of God'.[140] In the *Journal,* Fox constantly reiterates his total

---

[138] Fox, *Journal,* p. 9.
[139] Ibid., p. 14.
[140] Ibid., p. 27.

reliance upon this leading of the Spirit within to direct him in his prime mission of teaching the truths of God to all and sundry up and down the country and upon the power of God to enable him to do so; at Ulverston, for example, 'the Lord opened my mouth to speak',[141] and when Fox was invited in to 'John Wilkinson's steeple-house near Cockermouth', he writes how 'the Lord opened my mouth to declare His everlasting truth'.[142]

As the early-modern visionaries sought to hear God and live lives of biblical obedience, they experienced a range of interior supernatural revelations. These varied according to the individual, but all the visionaries emphasised the need to lead a life of purity and total obedience to God and the importance of rejecting the wiles of Satan. The purpose of all the visions and revelations was to change the believer into the likeness of Jesus through immersion in the Spirit, as described by the apostle Paul: 'But we all, with open face beholding as in a glass the glory of the Lord, are changed into the same image from glory to glory, even as by the Spirit of the Lord'.[143]

---

[141] Ibid., p. 72.
[142] Ibid., p. 83.
[143] 2 Cor. 3:18.

Chapter 3
Ecclesiology, Anti-Formalism and Individuality

As shown above, the early-modern visionaries were intensely focussed on a personal mission of being changed from within into the likeness of Jesus[144] and becoming increasingly more dedicated and effective agents of cosmic power.[145] Their zealous pursuit of these targets led to recurring tensions and conflicts as the inner promptings of the Spirit frequently ran counter to the expectations of culture and organised religion. Thus, although in many respects the environment of sixteenth-century Catholic Spain was quite dissimilar to that of seventeenth-century puritan England, many common difficulties and challenges were faced by the early-modern visionaries as they sought ways of maintaining their own integrity and inner equilibrium. These problematic areas will be considered in four broad categories. Firstly, serious spiritual and pragmatic issues were raised for the individual by the demands and restrictions of the organised Church, which frequently contradicted the leading of the Spirit. Secondly, at a time when the magical was commonly accepted, the Catholic Reformation and Interregnum Protestant churches offered a context in which supernatural experience could be acknowledged as a valid Christian

---

[144] 2 Cor. 3:18.

[145] Mills, M., in *Human agents of cosmic power in Hellenistic Judaism and the Synoptic tradition* (Sheffield, 1990), analyses biblical concepts of divine intervention through human agency, particularly focusing on Jesus.

pathway, but only subject to certain stringent checks and safeguards. Thirdly, statements in the biblical texts such as 'there is neither Jew nor Greek, there is neither bond nor free, there is neither male nor female, for ye are all one in Christ Jesus'[146] and personal visionary experience contradicted the rigid socio-economic roles imposed by gender, education and social class which also came into play in church structures. These issues common to society at large will be dealt with as part of the wider prophetic ministry of the visionaries in the next chapter. Finally, as the visionaries faced these conflicts they were obliged to innovate, take risks and create, and thus their own spiritual development was further accelerated.

Within the social and spiritual milieu of early-modern Europe, all members of society were expected to be professing and practising Christians; atheism and agnosticism were entirely unacceptable and regarded with horror. However, whilst Christianity was an obligatory social norm, the 'uncommitted majority'[147] did not feel led to think about it too deeply or prioritise their faith in their own lives. Churches, whether Protestant or Catholic, provided places of security and habit which offered some assurance of Divine approval as long as the rules and regulations of religious duty were performed more or less effectively. Hence the Church authorities had the responsibility of providing a dependable framework of belief and religious practice for the vast majority who had to be told what to do and what to believe because they were not particularly self-motivated and did not have the opportunity to develop a dynamic inner life. In addition, formal Church structures provided a sense of security and community; by complying with the roles offered within the structures of religious social relationships, the individual was guaranteed a defined and secure place in ritual and the group, without having to initiate or think. Firm boundaries were also considered necessary for the ill-

---

[146] Galatians 3:28.
[147] Durston, ''For the better humiliation of the people': public days of fasting and thanksgiving during the English Revolution', *The Seventeenth Century*, 7(1992), 142.

informed and misguided for whom faith could all too easily be confused with magical practice.

Therefore in order to protect and nurture the majority of basically unenthusiastic believers, both Catholic and Protestant Churches developed formal patterns of religious practice, hierarchies of priest or minister and people, and intellectual methods of scholasticism to delineate doctrinal boundaries. Furthermore, there were those in positions of responsibility who quite intentionally used ecclesiastical order as a way to control both the majority and the potentially dangerous enthusiastic minority. Archbishop Laud and his conservative Arminian clerics waged a 'systematic campaign against the godly and what they regarded as their highly subversive religious practices' in the late 1620s,[148] and in *The Crums of Comfort to Groans of the Spirit, the Second Part* of 1652 Michael Sparke ends his *Morning Prayer* of adoration:

> we beseech thee, remember the groaning griefs of all thy Churches, in all part. Root out, O dig up, destroy, and root out all that be not planted by thy hand, all Quakers, Shakers, Ranters, and Seekers, such as look not after thy Laws, or that live not according to thine Ordinances, but according to their own list, and wickedness of their will.[149]

This heavily structured and prescriptive formal religion was not enough for the small minority, both Catholic and Protestant, who were spiritually intense and whose primary focus was not outward form and observation but internalising and applying the Bible text. For them, in keeping with Jesus' teaching,[150] religious experience, assurance and emotional security were not to be resourced from external forms but the from Spirit within and in others, and a sense of community was built up primarily in Spirit-led emotional connections

---

[148] Durston, 'For the better humiliation of the people', pp. 130-2.

[149] Davies, H., *Worship and theology in England from Andrewes to Baxter and Fox, 1603-1690* (Princeton, 1975), pp. 72-73.

[150] Luke 17:21: 'the kingdom of God is within you'.

with other intense believers, not through formal structures. However, Catholic and Protestant visionaries dealt with their relationship to formal religion in different ways because of their different understanding of the nature of the Church. The Catholic belief in the necessity of belonging to the Catholic Church in order to attain salvation obliged Catholic visionaries to accommodate themselves to formal religion in a way which was not necessary for their Protestant counterparts, who saw salvation as coming directly and unmediated from God through grace, and the church as being the community of believers. Teresa, John and Mary accepted the sacramental system, veneration of Mary and other Catholic practices, but condemned their abuse when adopted as a substitute for real dedication to God in the Spirit. Many enthusiastic Protestants, on the other hand, were hostile to formalism as they saw it as the product of and a pathway into corrupt counterfeit religion and thus spiritually dangerous. The Leveller William Walwyn wrote of those who were satisfied with the observance of formal religion: 'it is in them traditional, and they are not truly religious; but mere moral Christians: utterly ignorant of the cleared Heavenly brightness, inherent in pure and undefiled Religion'.[151] In true biblical Christianity, 'a man is justified by faith without the deeds of the law',[152] so observance of rules and regulations and observance of the moral law as an end in itself had 'no place in Christian experience'.[153] As the believer was led by the Spirit working through the conscience, the moral and ethical Biblical requirements would be naturally fulfilled without legalistic reference to a set of rules. Any need for these regulations simply demonstrated that the apparent believer was not truly a believer. Those justified by Christ and

---

[151] Davis, J.C, 'Against formality: one aspect of the English Revolution', in *Transactions of the Royal Historical Society*, 6th series, 1 (1993), 281.

[152] Romans 3:28.

[153] Kendall, R.T., *The way of wisdom: patience in waiting on God* (Carlisle, 2002), p. 2.

led by the Spirit were now 'not without law to God, but under the law to Christ',[154] as 'the law of Christ *presupposes* that one is behaving himself morally, and takes one beyond the moral law'.[155] A true believer would zealously desire through grace to bring every single affection, motive and thought in line with the will of God. At the same time, the visionaries lived in an era when submission to authority was seen as true freedom:

> liberty and authority were not seen as antithetical but complementary... liberty in the common parlance of the seventeenth century was expressed in submission to an appropriate authority operating in a duly regulated way... formality reconciled liberty and authority.[156]

As long as structures were used to help the believer submit to the leading of the Spirit, they were desirable, but as soon as the believer had to submit to the forms instead of the Spirit, they were ungodly; in 1647 Peter Sterry preached to the Commons that 'Forms are sweet Helpes, but too severe Lords over our Faith'.[157] To this extent, Winstanley the Digger and Fox remained within the boundaries of Protestant belief and attitudes; rigorously rejecting the unbiblical libertine practices of the Ranters and unconverted, their moral standards were based on inner transformation not legalism, and they developed their own organisation and structure, albeit innovative, which followed Biblical guidelines of peace and order in submission to the Spirit. For Winstanley, a return to the parish church was appropriate when he felt it was time to move on from the Digger community and take up a more conventional lifestyle again. Thus both Catholic and Protestant visionaries, consistent with the teaching of the Scriptures, looked primarily to the Spirit within to give them

---

[154] 1 Cor. 9:21.
[155] Kendall, *The way of wisdom,* p. 3. Author's italics.
[156] Davis, 'Against formality', pp. 284, 287.
[157] Ibid., p. 274.

guidance and meet their needs rather than depending on the external agency of structures and legalism, whilst maintaining some kind of acceptance of church order in line with the Pauline teaching that 'God is not the author of confusion, but of peace'.[158]

This acceptance of religious order as necessary to salvation and holiness and protection from evil, shared by early-modern Catholics and Protestants, had to be expressed in different ways within the different traditions. Catholics were required to believe that salvation was through faith and works, the individual was assisted by grace transmitted through the seven sacraments, and that the eucharist involved the miracle of transubstantiation. The individual was to rely on the intermediary role of the religious hierarchy and draw on the accumulated merits of the saints and their advocacy, particularly the Virgin Mary, rather than depending solely on a direct line to God. Local patron saints of shrines in sixteenth-century Spain, for example, were chosen to plead for the local community; in 1597 the lay and clerical authorities in Madrid prayed during a plague, 'we humbly beseech [Saint Anne and Saint Roch] to be our patrons and advocates in the presence of God, placating the wrath of God we have so justly merited'.[159] The sacramental role of the ordained priesthood was perceived as indispensable and services were rigidly structured according to a defined rubric and had to be held in a sacred place. Teresa of Avila, John of the Cross and Mary Ward all demonstrated profound and consistent acceptance of all these requirements of formal religious practice yet insisted that outward observance alone was not enough; visionary experience found expression within the framework and extended beyond. In *The way of perfection,* Teresa insists that

> when people tell you that you are speaking with God by reciting the Paternoster and thinking of worldly things – well, words fail me. When you speak, as it is

---

[158] 1 Cor. 14:33.
[159] Christian, *Local religion in sixteenth-century Spain,* p. 55.

58

right for you to do, with so great a Lord, it is well that
you should think of Who it is that you are addressing,
and what you yourself are, if only that you may speak
to Him with proper respect.[160]

Obligatory private formal prayer and attendance at divine
office and at mass provided the context for Catholic visions
and ecstasy; Hsia states that 'all female mystical experiences
sanctioned by the Tridentine Church occurred in the setting of
the convent, usually in the chapel often during mass'.[161]
Teresa was embarrassed by her levitation 'as I was on my
knees, about to take communion',[162] Mary Ward was making
cords for Franciscan habits with other nuns at ten o'clock in
the morning when she was overwhelmed with a divine
revelation that 'came with such force that it annihilated and
reduced me to nothing'.[163] The spiritually directive writings
of John of the Cross were the outcome of monastic
contemplative prayer and his priestly 'preoccupation with the
business of government and the direction of souls'.[164] The
visionaries took opportunities to utilise apparent ecclesiastical
limitations on their freedom to suit their own agenda. The
papal bull *Circa pastoralis,* issued by Pius V in 1566,
reinforced the 1563 reform decree of Session XXV, Cap. V
of the Council of Trent, which called for the enclosure of all
female religious communities. This perfectly suited Teresa of
Avila's reforming zeal as it prohibited the aristocratic,
sociable and self-indulgent conventual life-style she had
experienced as a novice and demanded the strict asceticism
and enclosure she herself wished to promote. According to
Hsia, 'Teresa's success lay in her ability to reconcile two

---

[160] Teresa of Avila, *Way of perfection,* in *The complete works of Teresa of Avila, vol. 2,* E.A. Peers, trans. and ed. (London, 2002), p. 93.
[161] Hsia, R. Po-Chia, *The world of Catholic renewal 1540-1770* (Cambridge, 1998), p. 141.
[162] Teresa of Avila, *Life,* p. 137.
[163] Littlehales, *Mary Ward, pilgrim and mystic,* p. 50.
[164] Peers, *The complete works of Saint John of the Cross,* p. 1.

potentially conflicting interests in convent life: the male clerical impulse for control and the elite's appetite for honour'. The Catholic visionaries also had to contend with an ambivalent attitude from authorities towards interior prayer in the Catholic Reformation; from a spiritual point of view, it was encouraged, but too much individuality could become a threat to orthodoxy. By remaining within the boundaries of orthodoxy, the visionaries were able to make their own contribution to the formation of a distinctive Catholic Reformation spirituality, which included the key features of teaching on grace and justification, active works, and ascetic practice.[165]

For Winstanley and Fox, the Protestant context of the English Interregnum offered a divergence of possibilities in terms of formalism and anti-formalism. Both visionaries conformed entirely to Protestant ideals of interior experiential faith, a conversion experience of spiritual rebirth and a life dedicated to personal sanctification through reading the Scriptures and the agency of the Holy Spirit. These Protestant principles could be applied within strict Presbyterianism, the formal ritual of the Anglican Church or the radical sects. Winstanley and Fox were both strict formalists in terms of observing the moral laws and strongly rejected swearing, blasphemy and casual sex as allegedly practiced by the Ranters. In terms of religious practice, they took the same approach as Puritans such as William Perkins, whose writings 'generally emphasise soteriology not ecclesiology'.[166] Both also rejected formal structures of religious practice as distancing the believer from Christ; as Winstanley wrote, 'this seed of Christ then is to be seen within... therefore your public ministers bewitches you by telling you of a Saviour at a distance'.[167]

---

[165] Evenett, *The spirit of the Counter-Reformation* (Cambridge, 1998), p. 32.
[166] Kendall, R.T, *Calvin and English Calvinism to 1649* (Oxford, 1979), p. 1.
[167] Winstanley, *Fire in the bush*, p. 271.

In terms of a Scripture-based experiential faith, moral rectitude and radical religious practice, both visionaries were entirely in conformity with the principles of their own political leader, Oliver Cromwell. Cromwell's tolerant attitude to the radicals was motivated by his 'concern not to impose human authority between God's grace and the soul', and was founded on 'the faith that truth lay in the spirit rather than the institution – in spiritual power rather that ecclesiastical, confessional or liturgical form'.[168] Their choices about which existing structures to accept and which to reject were thus entirely in conformity with prevailing Calvinist principles; 'it has not come about by human perversity that the authority over all things on earth is in the hands of kings and other rulers, but by divine providence and human ordinance'.[169] Thus, although their beliefs and actions were often seen as atheistical and threatening to order by some in government or in the magistracy, Fox was protected by Cromwell. Furthermore, identical attitudes and aims were found in other separatist and radical groups such as the Levellers and the New Model Army as they also struggled to find the balance between following the directives of the Spirit and conforming to authority, a struggle which, when there was a conflict, could have only one outcome for those immersed in Calvinist religious culture. As Calvin himself had stated:

> the Lord, therefore, is the King of Kings, who, when he has opened his sacred mouth, must alone be heard, before and above all men; next to him we are subject to those men who are in authority over us, but only in him. If they command anything against him, let it go unesteemed.[170]

---

[168] Davis, J.C., 'Cromwell's religion', in *Oliver Cromwell and the English Revolution,* J. Morrill, ed. (Harlow, 1990), p. 191.
[169] Calvin, *Institutes,* p. 1489.
[170] Calvin, *Institutes,* p. 1520.

Finally, both Diggers and Quakers avoided an obsessive and formulaic rejection of all religious organisation. The Diggers had a peaceful, orderly and disciplined community life and the Quakers had definite principles for meetings; they

> dispensed with a professional ministry altogether and held completely unstructured meetings, at which both male and female members of the congregation could testify as and when the spirit moved them; they also developed their own simple marriage and burial services.[171]

Catholic and Protestant visionaries thus faced different problems in reconciling their own revelations with religious practice, although they had a common strength of purpose in maintaining their integrity and remaining within their own religious context. Some issues were the same for Catholics and Protestants. Both regarded the sacred space as being in God's creation of nature and within the individual Christian, whether they accepted ecclesiastical building and ritual as sacred or not. This was rooted in the Bible teaching that God was to be seen in his creation and that, like Jesus on the Mount of Olives, the believer was to pray in the natural environment. Fox and Winstanley habitually communed with God while in fields, orchards, woods and commons. Winstanley writes of his vision of the time,

> when men are sure of food and raiment, their reason will be ripe and ready to dive into the secrets of the creation, that they may learn to see and know God (the spirit of the whole creation) in all his works.[172]

John of the Cross took the novices at the priory of Los Martires in Granada into the countryside to as part of their

---

[171] Doran, S., and Durston, C., *Princes, pastors and people: the church and religion in England 1529-1689* (London, 1991), p. 30.
[172] Winstanley, *The Law of Freedom,* p. 365.

spiritual formation to develop their prayer life through *toda la hermosura de las cosas* –all the beauty of created things – and encouraged them to see all nature as praising God.[173]

The visionaries all had a special regard for other believers as being 'the temple of the living God'[174] and had a strong sense of community with and love for other Christians of a similarly intense spirit. Teresa describes how 'I always feel a great affection for those who direct my soul. I think of them as so truly taking the place of God that my mind is largely taken up with them'.[175] The correspondence of Teresa, John and Mary Ward similarly gives frequent evidence of intense love for their friends in religion. John became particularly attached to Teresa, his disciples Juan de Santa Ana and Juan Evangelista, and to Ana de Jesus and her nuns.[176] Winstanley's writings reiterate his love and concern for both his fellow-radicals and his opponents in ecstatic language, and for the Quakers this depth of personal attachment was fundamental to their sense of community, as can be seen in Fox's writings and in Quaker correspondence. Catholic and Protestant visionaries also agreed that it was essential to maintain high standards of virtuous behaviour, and that this was to come from within as a natural outcome of spirituality rather than as a result of keeping moralistic rules.

Both the Catholic and Protestant early-modern visionaries thus made strenuous attempts to accommodate themselves to their respective ecclesiastical context; however, their primary focus was to participate in the work of the Holy Spirit rather than to be spectators and recipients in formal religion. This often created real tensions and demanded perseverance, patience and creativity on the part of the visionaries, which in turn led to a greater self-awareness and spiritual and emotional development. In their own terms of seeking to make scripture a dynamic and internalised reality, this was perfectly consistent with biblical teaching that

---

[173] Brenan, *St John of the Cross*, pp. 53-54.
[174] 2 Cor. 6:16.
[175] Teresa, *Life*, p. 279.
[176] Brenan, *St John of the Cross,* p. 56.

all things work together for good to them that love God, to them who are the called according to his purpose. For whom he did foreknow, he also did predestinate to be conformed to the image of his Son, that he might be the firstborn among many brethren.[177]

As the visionaries sought to find the balance between ecclesiology and fidelity to the Spirit, they also had to establish their own relationship with doctrinal boundaries. Catholics had to define themselves in contrast with Lutheran and Reformed theology. They regarded tradition and scripture as of equal authority and Trent reaffirmed the medieval Augustinian position that justification comprised both the event of being made righteous through the work of Christ and the process of being made holy through the continuing work of the Holy Spirit within.[178] The individual had a choice as to how far to assist the work of sanctification in terms of self-denial. Grace was transmitted both directly and through the sacraments. Salvation was not possible outside the Catholic Church. Protestants believed in the sole authority of Scripture and that justification and sanctification were theologically distinct. Justification could not be accelerated by the individual's co-operation in terms of self-denial and good works, but these were a natural outcome of justification as this brought with it a desire to submit to the Spirit within. Grace was transmitted directly from God. For radical Protestants, salvation and sanctification were in principle possible in any godly community with biblical Trinitarian beliefs, although in practice Catholics were regarded as politically and ideologically dangerous. Belief in both double predestination and Arminianism was possible in seventeenth century England.

The writings and actions of the visionaries show a consistency with their own denominational beliefs. Teresa, for example, writes of her concern for the Lutherans trapped

---

[177] Romans 8:28-29.
[178] McGrath, *Christian theology,* p. 389.

in error.[179] Fox took Protestant scriptural belief in the Bible teaching of being born again in the Spirit to its extreme of tolerance, while reiterating that salvation was based solely on inner personal conversion:

> about the beginning of the year 1646, as I was going to Coventry, and entering towards the gate, a consideration arose in me, how it was said that all Christians are believers, both Protestants and Papists; and the Lord opened to me that, if all were believers, then they were all born of God, and passed from death to life, and that none were true believers but such; and though others said they were believers, yet they were not.[180]

However, whilst the visionaries acknowledged doctrinal boundaries, their beliefs and thought were not governed primarily by the imposition of these external systems but by their reading of Scripture enlightened by the Spirit within.[181] This may be understood in the context of the divergence of two fundamentally different styles of thinking which cut across denominations and were prominent in mid-sixteenth

---

[179] Teresa, *Way of perfection,* p. 3.

[180] Fox, *Journal,* p. 5.

[181] Dermot Fenlon, in *Heresy and obedience in Tridentine Italy: Cardinal Pole and the Counter Reformation* (Cambridge, 1972), pp. 18-19, describes this as applying to Italian humanists of the 1530, and later to members of the Curia in the persons of Contarini, Cortese, Pole and Morone. Fenlon says these humanists were 'impatient… with abstruse theological speculations: their theology was predominantly scriptural; it was addressed to the affections, not the intellect; and it was expressed in the language of persuasion rather than analysis. But in their pessimism about human nature, their preoccupation with the helplessness of man, and their insistence on the supremacy of faith, they were more akin to Luther than to Erasmus. Their most cherished ambition was to reform the Church and put an end to schism'. Fenlon goes on to state this spirit was also at work in Spain.

century Europe and Interregnum England: the evangelical in contrast to the scholastic, or inductive scriptural theology in contrast to deductive theology. Examples of these different thinking styles can be seen respectively in the Reformed theologians Calvin and Beza, and in the Catholics Cardinal Pole and the Jesuit Alfonso Salmeron. Alister McGrath states; 'Calvin's religious ideas, as presented in the 1559 *Institutes,* are *systematically arranged...* they are not *systematically derived* on the basis of a leading speculative principle'. Calvin focussed on the Bible, particularly on the historical events of Jesus Christ, and then examined its implications; his approach is analytic and inductive. Theodore Beza's approach is deductive and synthetic, that is, he begins from general principles and deduces the consequences.[182] As Calvinists, Lutherans and Catholics defined themselves the scholastic approach predominated in all confessions as theologians such as Beza and Bellarmine imposed rationally systematic arguments for their own dogmas: thus the Catholic Pole was obliged to change his approach by the authorities. Initially, 'he employed an exegetical approach, appealing to Scripture and to personal experience',[183] but he had to adjust his views in line with 'the ascendancy of the traditional Scholastic theological method at Trent'.[184] The influence of Scholasticism is clear in the development of Calvin's own brief reflections on predestination, written as part of a scriptural interpretation of the workings of grace, into articles of prescriptive dogma and hence the focus of animosity and disputes, such as those between Arminians and predestinarians at the Hampton Court conference.

Both Catholic and Protestant visionaries, by contrast, all shared the scripturally based inductive approach. However, they varied in their personal methods of dealing with the dominant scholastic doctrines. Teresa, John and Mary Ward acknowledged some value in systematic theology whereas

---

[182] McGrath, *Christian theology,* pp. 397-8.
[183] Fenlon, *Heresy and obedience in Tridentine Italy,* p. 189.
[184] Mullett, M., *The Catholic Reformation* (London, 1999), p. 49.

Fox and Winstanley strongly condemned it. Teresa reiterates her respect for learning and pragmatically uses it to protect herself – 'I did nothing without the approval of some learned men, so as in no way to infringe my obedience'[185] – whilst constantly refuting its usefulness in the higher reaches of prayer, 'preferring instruction from God himself'.[186] John of the Cross was highly trained in theology and Mary Ward's whole mission in life was to provide education based on the structured Jesuit model, yet both received their visions through the practice of affective scripturally based prayer. Fox and Winstanley showed extreme hostility to academic control of scriptural interpretation, as in their view this distorted it and excluded non-academics – Fox goes so far as to write of 'the black earthly spirit of the priests'.[187] Winstanley's and Fox's own writings and actions show a thorough knowledge of scripture and consistency of interpretation; thus Winstanley does not deal with issues of election and predestination from the perspective of either Beza's or Laud's analysis but from his own ecstatic experience and observation of the moving of grace and human co-operation.[188] Fox used knowledge of biblical Hebrew to make his case to magistrates: 'it is for Christ's sake I stand, for it is *lotish shabiun becoll daber'*.[189]

Both Catholic and Protestant early-modern visionaries shared their contemporaries' absolute acceptance of Biblical teaching on the reality of Satan as an aggressively antagonistic force in the life of the believer. For the majority, this was to be dealt with through the external agency of magical practice, whether provided by the church or not. Thus on occasion Teresa took advantage of the use of holy water when feeling under attack whereas the less spiritually

---

[185] Teresa, *Life,* p. 266.
[186] Ibid., p. 170.
[187] Fox, *Journal,* p. 23.
[188] Tyacke, N., *Anti-Calvinists: the rise of English Arminianism c.1590-1640* (Oxford, 1991), p. 70.
[189] Fox, *Journal,* p. 232.

orthodox might seek the help of cunning men or women. For Presbyterians and other Calvinists, protection was to be found in obedience to doctrine and trusting in the Word. For the visionaries, however, the forces of evil were to be engaged with internally, directly, personally and actively, in line with the example of prophets such as Elijah and the teaching of Paul.[190] This struggle was intrinsic to the sanctification of the visionary as each battle with the forces of evil became another big step in the changing of the person into the likeness of Jesus. Teresa attained a personal victory over fear, increased her trust in God and attained a higher level of understanding after one series of attacks.[191] Winstanley's entire theology of redemption and sanctification of the individual was based upon this inner struggle between good and evil and the triumph of the Seed of Christ over the dragon after painful turmoil. This is then projected into the outer world; the fight between good and evil in each person is enacted in the political realms of social, religious and academic organisation as those in whom the dragon is in the ascendant exploit and crush the weak. Those in whom Christ has the victory are to engage in winning over their enemies by love expressed in direct political action. Fox describes the victory he was given in the Spirit after he struggled with evil in the shape of depression, self-doubt and religious anxiety:

> I had been brought through the very ocean of darkness and death, and through and over the power of Satan, by the eternal, glorious power of Christ; even through that darkness was I brought, which covered-over all the world, and which chained down all, and shut up all in the death.[192]

It was only as a result of triumph over the forces of Satan that he was able to engage upon his life of ministry. For all the visionaries, the fight against evil was not merely an

---

[190] Ephesians 6:12.
[191] Teresa, *Life,* p. 174-183.
[192] Fox, *Journal,* p. 12.

external activity but an indispensable part of an inner process. Furthermore, as a corollary to the defeat of evil within the individual, more and more grace was expressed, first in the affections and then in actions. Thus virtue was not attained by complying with religious rules and regulations but was a natural overflowing of the Spirit within.

For all the visionaries, therefore, their relationship with formal religion was characterised by an inner liberty in the Spirit developed through obedience to the law of freedom in Christ as described in the Bible texts. Interaction with external forms varied according to social context and doctrinal affiliation, but inner experience was always consistent with Scripture.

Chapter 4
The Prophetic

For all the visionaries, the life of inner dedication to God and personal transformation through prayer led to prophetic action. This prophetic action always involved two aspects, as it did in the Biblical narrative accounts of the prophets, such as Isaiah, Jeremiah, John the Baptist and Jesus. This involved both the prophet's attempt to turn others to a closer obedience to God and action to bring about the kingdom of heaven on earth. According to the biblical narratives, this always provoked hostility and personal danger for the prophet, but seldom resulted in death, and always had some kind of successful outcome. Thus Teresa, John of the Cross, Mary Ward, Winstanley and Fox all had both a didactic ministry of the Word in teaching how to follow scriptural principles of repentance and inner sanctification, and a practical ministry in their various spheres of reformation of religious community, apostolic outreach, education, healing, political action and founding of new religious groups.

This reforming and missionary zeal was in all cases the product of inner union with God. Winstanley's activities were all rooted in the desire to act for God, 'for God is an active power, not an imaginary fancy'.[193] Mary Ward describes the inner push to prophetic action as being impossible to resist – 'divine love is like fire, which will not let itself be shut up, for it is impossible to love God and not to labour to extend His honour'.[194] It was not part of a career plan nor a logically structured objective analysis of what the visionary thought

---

[193] Winstanley, *The Law of Freedom,* p. 364.
[194] Ward, *The heart and mind of Mary Ward,* p. 57.

needed changing with an accompanying set of targets. The visionaries received their instructions from God by inner revelation as they pursued a life of prayer. They followed the biblical model, according to which prophecy was 'the *revealed word of God.* It was not the product of intellectual attainment or rational debate... it was the word of God delivered by God to man'. The function of prophecy was to remedy whatever was hindering the coming of the kingdom of God on earth, whether personal, ecclesiastical or political. Thus prophecy had 'an immediacy and a contemporary relevance that distinguished it from contemplative meditation or speculative philosophy'.[195] However, whereas in the Hebrew Bible God had chosen only a few individuals for the task, in the New Testament texts all Christians had the potential to prophesy and if a person had the gift of prophecy this was to be used 'according to the proportion of faith'.[196] The natural consequence of the visionaries' dedication a life of faith in the Spirit was a fulfilment in them of the prophet Joel's words repeated in Acts 2:17-18:

> in the last days, saith God, I will pour out my Spirit upon all flesh: and your sons and daughters shall prophesy, and your young men shall see visions, and your old men shall dream dreams: and on servants and on my handmaidens I will pour out in those days of my Spirit; and they shall prophesy.

As in the biblical text, the prophetic ministry of each visionary was determined by what was needed in the circumstances; for example, Amos stressed the justice of God, Hosea the loving-kindness and mercy of God, and Isaiah emphasised God's moral righteousness and ethical against ritualistic requirements. All followed the same prophetic principles, with outcomes suited to context.

---

[195] Hill, Clifford, *Prophecy past and present* (Guildford, 1995), p. 12.
[196] Romans 12:6.

In this prophetic role, the visionaries acted only on direct revelation from God as to the tasks they were to fulfil. Fulfilling these was often directly counter to their own ease and prosperity and the final outcome was not made clear; by definition, as the prophetic task was to correct whatever was wrong, they were invariably counter-cultural and in human terms appeared at best irrational and foolish. Consequently, it was impossible for the visionaries to lay plans in the ordinary sense and this obliged them to rely even further on God for the next step by persevering in prayer. As they were focussed on leading their entire lives in submission to the leading of the Spirit, it was essential for the visionaries to be absolutely sure that they were actually hearing God and not, as the Bible warns, false prophecies emanating from a fertile human imagination or from evil spirits.[197] For them, although God's commands were often difficult to follow, they were clear; firstly, God would never contradict Scripture, secondly, the visionary would ask for discernment and continue to pray until revelation was given, and thirdly, feelings of joy and peace would accompany God's truth whereas sorrow and dejection would accompany evil spirits. Furthermore, the prophet had to be detached from all personal desires for success or achievement or this would distort the message received from the Spirit within.

An aspect of prophetic activity was the ability to endure the spiritual and emotional desert experience of total isolation, in conformity with the biblical prophets, as the visionary pioneered and innovated in prayer and in practical life. Whether this included a feeling of separation from God or a more intense experience of the presence of the Spirit, the visionary had to be able to withstand difficulty and resistance without human support whilst applying new interpretations of the Bible to organisational structures. This always led to acting alone and often to periods of imprisonment. However, after the initial phase of total isolation from all support except that of the Spirit, the visionaries all attracted a small group of like-minded individuals who, although they were not always

---

[197] Hill, referring to 1 Cor:12 in *Prophecy past and present,* p. 202.

available to provide a stable social context, provided emotionally, spiritually and intellectually intimate connections. In their prophetic role as innovators, pioneers and independent thinkers, the visionaries were neither hermits nor enmeshed in a legalistically structured static community.

The primary function of the Biblical prophet was to call the individual to repentance in terms of returning whole-heartedly to the God of the Scriptures and rejecting sinful ways. Teresa, John, Mary, Fox and Winstanley all obeyed the directive of the Spirit within to dedicate their lives to this ministry of rebuke and edification, repeating John the Baptist's call to 'repent and believe the Gospel'. Fox states in the *Journal*, 'I was sent to turn people from darkness to the light, that they might receive Jesus Christ'.[198] Teresa and John of the Cross did this primarily in their writings on prayer, in letters and in spiritual direction of those in community and like-minded co-religionists. Mary Ward did so in her apostolic ministry to lay adults, her educational activities for children and in her teaching ministry to others within her own community. Winstanley actively exhorted those in political power to repent and turn to God in his broadsheets, and built up his own fellow Diggers into a community. Fox had an extensive public hedge-preaching ministry and engaged in correspondence to exhort and rebuke. Like the biblical prophets, the visionaries taught this message both in words and by the consistent example of their lifestyle of continuing sanctification through fidelity and obedience.

This ministry was intensely personal and fundamentally educational, having as its objective the enabling of the individual to relate directly and effectively with God and thus co-operating with the sanctifying work of the Holy Spirit rather than relying on religious systems to do the work for them. This educational agenda was targeted according to the environment of the visionary and the needs of those around them, following the pattern of biblical prophetic ministry. Thus Teresa's educational programme was the exhortation and instruction of fellow literate Catholics, particularly those

---

[198] Fox, *Journal,* p. 20.

of an ascetic and mystical disposition. John of the Cross had a very similar ministry and extended it to the urban poor, including teaching poor children in Avila to read and write.[199] Mary Ward had the prophetic task of educating adults and girls, specifically but not exclusively recusant and apostate Catholics. Significantly, this educational programme included Latin; this enabled the girls to read the Vulgate and follow the Latin Mass with understanding and liberated them to read about their faith independently (though within bounds set by the Church) beyond the vernacular. The Catholic visionaries all had a dual focus of encouraging the individual to develop a personal relationship with God, not relying solely on outer forms, whilst reinforcing the need to submit to Catholic doctrine, avoid heresy and remain part of the Catholic Church. This was perfectly in accordance with Catholic teaching on salvation through both faith and sanctification and the impossibility of achieving salvation outside the Church.

Winstanley's educational focus was those in political power and all other literate adults with a degree of intellectual capacity through his broadsheets and his court appearances, and the formation of children in his educational plans outlined in *The Law of Freedom.* Winstanley's pedagogical vision for children was to train, edify and enable them to grow up to fulfil their godly role in the community as adults. They were to be trained in practical skills to equip them to lead useful, honest and prosperous adult lives, in history to give prophetic understanding of the world around them (that is, to interpret events in the light of biblical teaching), and in reading to understand the Word and liberate the individual from bondage to clergy and lawyers.[200] For Fox, the main thrust of his ministry was teaching through preaching to groups and individuals, so that people would be turned to God and 'come

[199] Kavanaugh, K., OCD, and Rodriguez, O., OCD, trans and eds, 'Biographical sketch', in *The collected works of St John of the Cross* (Washington, 1991), p. 17.
[200] Winstanley, *The Law of Freedom,* pp. 361-366.

into subjection to the Spirit of God, and grow up in the image and power of the Almighty', and 'come to know the hidden unity in the Eternal Being'.[201] For the Protestants Winstanley and Fox, the purpose of their educational ministry was identical to that of the Catholics in terms of seeking to enable the individual's own access to God. However, whereas the Catholics saw this as complementary to integrating the person into a religious system, the Protestants perceived the shoring up of formal religion as being potentially destructive to the individual. Salvation was through faith alone, the sanctification which followed was the work of the Holy Spirit and membership of existing visible ecclesiastical organisations was not only superfluous but could be harmful, as a system of access through a priestly elite demanded blind obedience from the masses which was *per se* contradictory to obedience to God. For all the visionaries therefore the message of personal repentance and a life of sanctification was the key issue, whilst the question of how this connected with the individual's relationship with church structure varied between Catholics and Radical Protestants.

As part of their prophetic ministry, Teresa, John, Mary, Fox and Winstanley all shared the passion of the biblical prophets to reform their own religious structures from within. The Catholic visionaries accepted the authority of hierarchical structures and focussed their energy on reform of patterns of religious community. Teresa founded first St Joseph's and then other convents of the Reform and John reformed Carmelites into a prophetic model. Mary's Institutes were modelled on the Society of Jesus, with the community directly accountable to the Pope not a bishop, non-enclosed, and the Office not said in common. Winstanley's writings show an incessant persuasive intensity for his readers to abandon the false religion of clerics and outward forms, his life with the Diggers modelled the prophetic ideal of a small community of believers living biblical principles of justice and peace whilst other writings give detailed action plans on how to

---

[201] Fox, *Journal,* p. 17.

bring a godly society into reality.[202] A major focus of Fox's preaching ministry was the call to reject the false religions of the steeple-houses and for true believers to gather together and form the true church of those who were filled with the Spirit and listened to and obeyed the inner light.

This apostolic zeal was not limited to those already within church structures. The visionaries took to heart the biblical directive that God does not desire the death of a sinner but repentance. Teresa had a strong desire to convert the heathen and she felt deep compassion for the heretical condition of Lutherans, earnestly desiring to bring them back into the one true Catholic Church in which they would find salvation.[203] Mary Ward had a mission to apostate Catholics (who had wilfully placed themselves outside the scope of salvation), to heretical Protestants and to those on the fringes – 'the prisoners, the sick, and the dying'.[204] Winstanley and Fox had a special sympathy for those oppressed by structures, ill-equipped to function within existing models of church and therefore effectively excluded from active participation in mainstream religion. It was those who prospered within the system who needed rebuke and repentance, but to those forcibly shut out from full participation by rank, gender or education they proclaimed the prophetic message of Isaiah: the Sovereign Lord will gather the exiles, the outcasts, the eunuchs and the foreigners, and all who love and serve him and hold fast to his covenant so that 'my house shall be called an house of prayer for all people'.[205] Fox's missionary zeal led him to evangelise Barbados, Jamaica, New England, Carolina and Virginia.[206] He later also made missionary trips to the Netherlands.[207]

---

[202] Winstanley, *The Law of Freedom,* pp. 314-389.

[203] Teresa, *Way of perfection,* p. 3.

[204] Littlehales, *Mary Ward: pilgrim and mystic,* p. 66.

[205] Isaiah 56:7.

[206] Fox, *Journal*, pp. 271-310.

[207] Stephen, L., and Lee, S. eds, *Dictionary of national biography vol. VII* (Oxford, 1968), p. 560.

The practical reforming zeal of the Catholic visionaries was focussed on religious community. Since for zealous Protestants the whole of society was religious community, Winstanley and Fox felt a prophetic call to reform political and social structures in a profoundly radical sense. Winstanley's prophetic vision was that of a godly society based on scriptural truth, justice and peace. It was internally consistent, based on biblical principles, systematically and logically presented in *The Law of Freedom* and was the basis for his direct action on St George's Hill, his personal conduct, his moral attitudes and his political pamphleteering activities. This programme of reform was intelligently and logically presented but was the product of the prophetic interpretation of biblical truth ecstatically revealed to Winstanley by the Spirit within; as the dragon of deceptive imagination struggled to control humanity, unrighteousness, misery and injustice ruled in the political and social spheres. This was to be overcome by the King of righteousness taking the victory in men's hearts and through them bringing a proper and just order into society at large:

> this great Leveller, Christ our King of righteousness in us, shall cause men to beat their swords into ploughshares and spears into pruning hooks, and nations shall learn war no more; and every one shall delight to let each other enjoy the pleasures of the earth, and shall hold each other no more in bondage.[208]

Winstanley's prophetic role was to translate this vision into a practical action plan with specifics, as laid out in *The Law of Freedom*.[209] Fox did not have a political programme as such but worked unceasingly to confront injustice by engaging in dialogue with those in authority. This prophetic direct action had the dual effects of causing the individual to be 'convinced' and bringing about justice, mercy and peace

---

[208] Winstanley, *A New-year's gift for the Parliament and Army,* p. 204.
[209] Winstanley, *The Law of Freedom*, pp. 294-389.

in the social context, as was the case when Fox was in prison in Derby in 1651:

> there was a young woman in the jail for robbing her master of some money. When she was to be tried for her life, I wrote to the judge and to the jury about her, shewing them how contrary it was to the law of God in time to put people to death for stealing, and moving them to shew mercy. Yet she was condemned to die, and a grave was made for her; and at the time appointed she was carried forth to execution. Then I wrote a few words, warning all people to beware of greediness or covetousness, for it leads from God, but that all should fear the Lord and avoid all earthly lusts, and prize their time while they have it: this I gave to be read at the gallows. And though they had her upon the ladder with a cloth bound over her face, ready to be turned off, yet they did not put her to death, but brought her back again to prison: and in the prison she afterwards came to be convinced of God's everlasting truth.[210]

Fox followed this principle of prophetic dialogue with authority in his meeting with the Lord Protector in 1654 while in custody: when Cromwell 'said we quarrelled with priests, whom he called ministers', Fox answered with biblical authority that

> if we own the prophets, Christ, and the apostles, we cannot hold up such teachers, prophets, and shepherds as the prophets Christ, and the apostles declared against; but we must declare against them by the same power and Spirit'. After this meeting Cromwell ordered Fox to be "at liberty".[211]

As the visionaries continually referred to the biblical texts and listened to the Holy Spirit within, their personal

---

[210] Fox, *Journal,* p. 38.
[211] Fox, *Journal,* pp. 104-106.

relationships and attitudes were modelled differently from those prevailing in their social and political contexts. This is particularly noticeable in issues of gender, education and social rank as these were considered to be defining factors of personality, spheres of action and personal association in the contemporary social and political milieu. This difference was not rooted in an anachronistic programme of proto-Marxist or radical feminist ideology but was the outcome of single-minded focus on the scriptural narrative; the biblical prophets were male and female and from a variety of backgrounds – King Josiah saved his kingdom from disaster only by following the prophetess Huldah's instructions, Isaiah moved in court circles, Amos was a shepherd; and the early church as described in the New Testament texts forbade distinction on grounds of gender or social status. Thus Teresa was from a wealthy and respectable family whereas John of the Cross was brought up by a poor widowed mother of lowly origins who had to travel from town to town to find work; John was highly educated, Teresa was not; Teresa was female, John was male. All these otherwise insuperable differences became irrelevant within the intense spiritual intimacy which developed between them and their small group of friends as they engaged on the path to union with God and spiritual and practical reform of the Carmelites. Teresa insisted that in the Reformed convents there were to be no distinctions by rank between lay and choir sisters as was customary; in Christ Jesus all were to be equal and the superior was to be the first to sweep the floor.[212] Mary Ward made every effort to submit to Tridentine guidelines of Catholic femininity by joining the enclosed Poor Clares. However, as she sought to be obedient to God's revealed directives in her visions she found herself building a community modelled on the male structures of the Jesuits where authority was invested in the superior – who was now female – and where distinction between social rank of lay sister and choir sister was replaced by the three functional grades of those in authority, teachers, and lay

---

[212] Kavanaugh and Rodriguez, *The collected works of St John of the Cross,* p.16.

sisters. Mary's friends and associates were both male and female and not limited to her own rank of origin, which was gentry. For all her energetic conscious striving to submit to the male hierarchical priestly authority of the Catholic Church, Mary Ward found herself on occasion vigorously asserting biblical principles of gender equality in the Spirit in spite of herself:

> I would to God that all men understood this obvious truth that women if they will to be perfect, and if men would not make women believe they can do nothing, and that we are mere women, we might do great matters.[213]

Winstanley's prophetic message was *ipso facto* that of 'Jesus Christ the saviour of all men', 'the greatest, first and truest Leveller that ever was spoke of in the world', who abolished all distinctions of persons, whether of rank, education, wealth or property ownership.[214] Winstanley does not give much focus to gender issues and in his visionary re-structuring of society and in *The Law of Freedom* he assumes that positions of authority will be held by males. However, he does insist that girls should be well-educated, including reading, and that women should be treated with respect in their relationships with men; the 'Laws for marriage' specify that men and women should be free to marry for love regardless of birth, if a woman becomes pregnant by a man 'he shall marry her', and if a man rapes a woman 'he shall be put to death'.[215] Fox took the scriptural teachings on equality in the Spirit to heart in all areas of life, giving women led by the inner light complete equality with male friends in preaching, teaching and evangelising, and encouraging all to move beyond restrictions of education, rank and income as the Spirit rendered these hindrances entirely unnecessary.

---

[213] Ward, *The heart and mind of Mary Ward,* p. 38.

[214] Winstanley, *A New-Year's gift for the Parliament and Army,* p. 199.

[215] Winstanley, *The Law of Freedom,* p. 388.

Healing, learning and social interaction were all now to be enlightened by the Spirit, not conformed to corrupt worldly tradition.

This freedom from earthly definition of relationships included blood ties, which were of key importance in early-modern Europe in defining status and those available for affective relationships. Jesus, on the other hand, taught that whoever does the will of God is his mother and brother and sister, as all true believers are children of the one Heavenly Father. This fictive kinship amongst all those filled with the Spirit as against biological kinship is a major characteristic of the New Testament texts; Christians are referred to as brothers and sisters, Paul describes Timothy and Titus as his children, and says that Rufus' mother is his own.[216] Paul goes so far as to tell Philemon to welcome back a runaway slave whom he is entitled to execute 'not now as a servant, but above a servant, a brother beloved', because he has converted thanks to Paul's teaching: 'I beseech thee for my son Onesimus, whom I have begotten in my bonds'.[217] Teresa, John and Mary Ward all applied this biblical teaching on fictive kinship as part of their prophetic ministry; this was an aspect of Catholic tradition for those in community but had not always been observed consistently. Generally speaking, for Protestants the onus was on putting the earthly family first and focussing affection and spirituality within it. Winstanley, however, makes no mention of his birth family but writes with great affection of his fellow − Diggers. Fox writes that at first he separated himself from his blood relatives in order to immerse himself in the Spirit, as Jesus commanded, but after having been through this process, he went on to write with great warmth of both his family and his brothers and sisters in Christ, the other Friends.

Occasionally, the prophet would predict the future. This could be to point out the harmful consequences of not turning away from a sinful course of action, to show the blessing that would result from a return to God, or simply to confirm the

---

[216] Romans 16:13.
[217] Philemon, vv. 16, 10.

visionary's prophetic ability. Teresa describes how 'I have been told things two or three years beforehand that have afterwards been fulfilled and so far none of them has proved untrue'.[218] Mary Ward is shown in picture forty-five of the *Painted Life* receiving a predictive prophetic revelation;

> when Maria travelled for the first time to Munich, God had made known to her, as she told her companions not far from the Isarberg, that His Highness the Elector would give them a comfortable dwelling in his city and annual support, which happened soon after their arrival.[219]

Fox states that 'many openings I had of several things which would be large to utter'.[220] These 'openings I had from the Lord' were 'not only of divine and spiritual matters, but also of outward things, relating to the civil government'. Early in 1653 he prophesied:

> being one day in Swarthmoor Hall, when Judge Fell and Justice Benson were talking of the news in the News Book, and of the Parliament then sitting, which was called the Long Parliament, I was moved to tell them that before that day two weeks the Parliament should be broken up, and the speaker plucked out of his chair.[221] This was a prophecy which proved correct.

Consistent with the biblical accounts of prophetic intervention, the visionaries also acted as agents of God to heal the sick and liberate those oppressed by evil spirits. Part of this ministry was the gift of discernment which was necessary to diagnose spiritual disease and bring the remedy

---

[218] Teresa, *Life,* p. 174.

[219] Peters, *Mary Ward: a life in contemplation*, p. 430 for text, Littlehales, *Mary Ward: pilgrim and mystic,* plate 16, for print of panel.

[220] Fox, *Journal,* p. 81.

[221] Ibid., p. 86.

of repentance. Teresa describes how her prayers for healing miracles were granted: as she was 'earnestly importuning the Lord to restore the sight of a person who was almost blind', she was granted a vision of Jesus telling her that 'anything you ask of me I promise you to do', and within a week 'the Lord restored that person's sight'. On another occasion, Teresa visited and prayed for a relative was ill with 'a very painful disease', and 'on the very next day my relative was free from pain'.[222] This ministry of miraculous healing through prayer extended to spiritual malaise; 'in answer to my prayers, the Lord has very often delivered souls from grave sins and brought others to great perfection'.[223] Sister Maria stated that when surgeons removed John's bandages they 'cured other sick persons by applying them to them',[224] just as Paul's handkerchiefs had done.[225] According to Ana de San Alberta, John 'had a particular gift of exorcism' and she cites how he exorcised a nun in Avila.[226] Mary Ward also exercised miraculous charismata: she cured one of Countess Palffy's daughters of fever,[227] and according to panel 26 of the *Painted Life* a 'dangerous mutiny' was quelled through her prayers.[228] Fox often used discernment to speak to and heal inner sickness:

> there came... another woman, and stood at a distance from me, and I cast mine eye upon her, and said, "Thou hast been a harlot;" for I perfectly saw the condition

---

[222] Teresa, *Life,* p. 295.

[223] Ibid., p. 296.

[224] Maria de Jesus, 'Letter dated April 11, 1614', in *The complete works of St John of the Cross*, p. 326.

[225] Acts 19:11-12; God wrought special miracles by the hands of Paul: so that from his body were brought unto the sick handkerchiefs or aprons, and the diseases departed from them, and the evil spirits went out of them.

[226] Ana de San Alberto, 'An account by M. Ana de San Alberto', in *The complete works of Saint John of the Cross,* p. 349.

[227] Peters, *Mary Ward: a world in contemplation,* p. 464.

[228] Ibid., p. 162.

and life of the woman. The woman answered and said many could tell her of her outward sins, but none could tell her of her inward. Then I told her heart was not right before the Lord, and that from the inward came the outward. This woman came afterwards to be convinced of God's truth, and became a Friend.[229]

This power to heal spiritual and psychological disorder was manifested when Fox 'came out of Carlisle prison' and met with a 'mad woman that was sometimes very desperate', and 'the Lord's power ran through her' so that she recovered. In Cumberland, Fox met with a woman who 'was distracted and very desperate, attempting at times to kill her children and her husband', but after Fox was 'moved of the Lord God to speak to her', she recovered; 'the Lord's power wrought through her and she went home well'.[230] Fox continues with an account of an eleven year old boy who was bent double and was so infirm that 'all the doctors had given over' and 'his father and grandfather feared he would have died;' Fox 'was moved of the Lord God to lay my hands upon him and speak to him', and the boy was healed and three years later 'he was grown to be a straight, full youth'.[231] The *Book of miracles* contains multiple accounts of healings, such as smallpox (Kent and London), convulsions (Cornwall), ulcers (London), fever (Wellingborough and Bristol) and ague (Bristol).[232] When it was too late for healing, Fox was able to comfort the bereaved by mental vision and spiritual perception given in the power of the Spirit: when a child had died, 'after the spirit of the Child appeared to me and there was a mighty substance of a glorious life in that child and I bid her mother be content, for it was well'.[233] Thus Fox, like

---

[229] Fox, *Journal,* p. 86.

[230] Ibid., p. 92.

[231] Fox, *Journal,* p. 93.

[232] Fox, *Book of miracles,* H.J. Cadbury, ed. (London, 2002), pp. 111-113.

[233] Fox, *Journal,* p. 86.

Teresa, was given revelation of the dead; in this case, the vision was given for the benefit of the mother, whereas Teresa's were to guide her in her own prayers.[234]

From the textual evidence therefore it can be seen that for all the early-modern visionaries the commitment to prayer, inner transformation in accordance with what they believed to be the work of the Holy Spirit, and obedience to the directives of God always led to prophetic action. The precise form varied according to the circumstances and mission of the individual; sometimes it involved practical reform, sometimes dissemination of a prophetic message, and sometimes supernatural activity. It could be in accordance with political and ecclesiastical authority but often involved opposition. It was always in accordance with Scripture and in submission to the Spirit within, and was directed towards bringing about God's justice and peace on earth within the individual and in society. In every case, the visionary was seeking to fulfil the agency of God in the same task given first to Isaiah and then to Jesus:

> the Spirit of the Lord is upon me, because he hath anointed me to preach the gospel to the poor; he hath sent me to heal the broken-hearted, to preach deliverance to the captives, and recovering of sight to the blind, to set at liberty them that are bruised, to preach the acceptable year of the Lord.[235]

---

[234] Teresa, *Life,* pp. 292-293.

[235] Luke 4:13: the text of Isaiah 61:1-2, read aloud by Jesus in the synagogue on his return from the forty days in the wilderness, at the beginning of his ministry.

Chapter 5
Conclusion

The early-modern visionaries considered here were all motivated by a desire to make the biblical narrative their own personal discourse. They internalised the biblical teachings on inner transformation into the likeness of Jesus through union with God, the need to pray without ceasing and obedience to the leadings of the Holy Spirit within. Listening to God could lead to visions, locutions and revelations, but these were never sought for their own sake and were considered to be dangerous if anything other than mental or interior. The religious experience of the visionaries extended beyond what was offered in formal religion and each individual had to find their own resolution to the tensions of relating to the establishment. Visionary experience always resulted in action to attempt to bring about what was believed to be God's will on earth, to change individuals, the Church and political structures; this action took both everyday and supernatural forms. The outer expression of these common characteristics varied according to the individual and the social context, and there was some variation between Catholic and Protestants. Catholics submitted themselves to Church hierarchy, engaged in Catholic religious practice such as veneration of the Virgin Mary, saw membership of the Catholic Church as essential to salvation, and regarded academic theological study as valid, whereas the Protestant visionaries did not accept any of these principles. Catholics referred to the Vulgate, the Protestants to the Geneva Bible and the King James' translation. Catholics submitted all their visions to Catholic authority, whereas Protestant visionaries accepted only the direct authority of the Holy Spirit. Catholics used ascetic practice to sharpen up their spirituality, but Fox and Winstanley did not require self-mortification beyond difficulties resulting from a life of obedience to the Spirit, such as imprisonment. In the context of the early-modern emphasis placed on the definition of the individual by doctrinal differences, gender, social rank and biological family, however, what is most striking about these individuals is their shared vision and common evangelical commitment to leading a life of fidelity to the Spirit within; they could say, with Paul,

> I am crucified with Christ: nevertheless I live; yet not I, but Christ liveth in me: and the life which I now live in the flesh I live by the faith of the Son of God, who loved me, and gave himself for me.[236]

---

236 Galatians 2:20.

Appendix
Biographical Sketches

Teresa of Avila

Teresa was born in 1515 in Avila. She had two sisters and nine brothers; her grandfather was Jewish. Her mother died when Teresa was sixteen and Teresa was sent as a boarder to the school run by the local Augustinian sisters. At twenty-one she joined the Carmelites and suffered bad health until the age of forty. She attempted the prayer of quiet, following the writings of the Franciscan Francisca de Osuna, but did not make much progress until 1555, when she read Augustine's *Confessions.* As a result of her spiritual experiences she founded St Joseph's Convent, the first of the Reformed communities, in 1562, following a strict regime of prayer and dedication but allowing for recreation and friendship between the sisters. Her first book, the *Life,* was finished in 1565. Teresa's vision was for the Discalced Reformed Carmelites to grow and then separate from the Unreformed Observants; for the rest of her life she encountered both opposition and support from influential and wealthy people. In 1567, Teresa founded the convent at Medina del Campo; while there she met John of the Cross, with whom she discussed the foundation of the first male monastery of the Reform. Between 1568 and 1576 she founded eight convents. In 1571, she became prioress at the convent of the Incarnation in Avila. From 1576 to 1580, strife within the Order prevented new foundations; in 1577 there were violent scenes at the election of a prioress at the convent of the Incarnation in Avila, and nuns voting for Teresa were excommunicated. Teresa finished the *Interior Castle* in November 1577. In 1579, she

was authorised to resume visitatio
sent the *Way of perfection* to th
1580, the Discalced Reform was
province by a Bull of Gregory XIII
convents. In 1581, the separation o
Carmelites became operative; Teresa
Soria and later that year was elected p.
Avila. In 1582, she founded the convent .
the *Foundations*, and at the command of
to visit the Duchess of Alba de Tormes,
October 4.

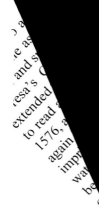

John of the Cross

John of the Cross was born in 1542 in Fontive
father was from a wealthy family who disinherited him
he married a poor weaver; John was the youngest of th
three children. His father died when he was two; this reduced
the family to poverty and John's brother died. His mother
resumed weaving in Medina del Campo, where John entered
a school providing practical apprenticeships for poor children.
John showed no aptitude for these, instead assisting the
director of the school at the sacristy of the Augustinian nuns
and supporting the administrator of the hospital as nurse and
alms-collector. At seventeen he attended the Jesuit school
where he learned grammar, rhetoric, Latin, Greek and Spanish
classics. In 1563, he joined the Carmelites, went to Salamanca
University and studied philosophy, in which he excelled. In
1567, he was ordained priest and visited Medina, where he
met Teresa, who was considering whether the Reformed
Carmelite life should be extended to the friars. She was 52, he
was 25. He was inspired by her vision, and after he had
finished his studies the following year John travelled with her
and a small group to Valladolid, where she intended to make
a new foundation. From August to October, Teresa became
John's spiritual teacher; he then left Valladolid to convert into
a monastery a farmhouse Teresa had acquired for her first
friars. In 1568, John embraced the new unmitigated Carmelite
Rule and in the following year novices arrived. The work

bigger house and two new foundations were
a house of studies for new friars with John as
spiritual director. John became spiritual director of
Carmelites in Avila in 1572; this ministry was
to people in the city and he also taught poor children
and write. The Observant Carmelites arrested him in
after which he was released at the Nuncio's orders, and
in December 1577, after the Nuncio died. John was
imprisoned in a small cell, flogged and lived on bread and
water until he escaped in 1578. While still a fugitive he
became vicar of the monastery on El Calvario. He was rector
of the Carmelite College in Baeza 1579-82. He became
director of the nuns at Beas and became spiritually close to
the prioress, Ana de Jesus. In 1580, the Holy See allowed the
Discalced Friars to erect an autonomous province and in 1582
John was elected prior of the monastery near Granada. He
continued spiritual direction of friars, nuns, clergy and lay
people and started his work as a writer. In 1585, he became
vicar provincial of Andalusia and founded seven new
monasteries. In 1588, he became third councillor to the vicar
general for the Discalced and returned to Segovia, where he
was prior. He concluded the *Living Flame of Love* and
devoted his time to prayer and manual work. Conflict arose
within the Discalced and John was sent to the monastery of
La Penuela, where he prepared for a mission to Mexico. He
died in 1591.

Mary Ward

Mary Ward was born in 1585 in Yorkshire into a recusant
gentry family. In 1606, she joined the Poor Clares in St Omer
as an out-sister; this role was not suitable for her and together
with thirteen others she founded a monastery for English Poor
Clares. She had a revelation that she was to live in the world
and in 1609 she left the convent, went to London and engaged
in apostolic work. After another vision she returned to St
Omer to found a boarding school for English girls and a day
school for local children. In 1611, she had a revelation that
she was to found a community based on the Jesuit model.

Houses were opened in Flanders and from 1614 there were always some members in London. A request was sent to Pope Paul V for approbation of the community Institutes. Between 1616 and 1621 houses were founded in Liege, Cologne and Trier. In 1621, Mary had an audience with Pope Gregory XV and she opened schools in Rome, Naples and Perugia. Mary's supporters included Jesuits, senior clerics and influential lay people, but as a pioneer in non-enclosure and government by a female General Superior, she also had many enemies. In 1625, the Regular Congregation issued a Decree to suppress the English Ladies in Italy and the houses in Rome and Perugia were closed. In 1626, Mary went to Munich; in 1627 Maximilian I made an Enactment in favour of the English Ladies and Mary founded houses in Vienna and Pressburg. However, the Congregation ordered the Nuncios to suppress the 'Jesuitesses'. In 1629, Mary returned to Rome to petition Urban VIII. In 1630, the houses in Saint-Omer, Liege, Cologne, and Trier were suppressed. A Bull of Suppression was signed by Pope Urban VIII in January 1631; in February Mary was imprisoned in Munich by the Inquisition but released in March. In 1632, she was summoned to Rome by Urban, who cleared her of heresy and permitted her to re-open a school in Rome. She left Rome in 1637 and went to Paris, Spa, Liege, Cologne, Stavelot, Bonn and Antwerp. In 1639, she went to Saint-Omer and then London, setting up a large household and taking pupils. In 1641, Mary moved with most of her community to Yorkshire, where she died in 1645.

Gerrard Winstanley

Winstanley was baptised in the parish church in Wigan in 1609; he probably came from a family of artisans. From 1630 to 1638 Winstanley was apprenticed in London to a devout, well-educated widow, Sarah Gater of the Merchant Taylor's Company. He then became a householder and shopkeeper in Old Jewry and in 1640 he married Susan King. Winstanley states in his tracts that he had long been a conventional worshipper and a 'strict goer to Church;' he was an active member of the parish church and in 1643 he took the Solemn

League and Covenant for the defence of the Protestant religion. By 1642 Winstanley was in difficulties due to unpaid debts owed to him and by the end of 1643 he had to close his business. He moved to live close to his wife's family in Cobham, Surrey, became a grazier and was a householder in Street Cobham in 1646. In 1647, the harvest was poor and Surrey experienced a dramatic increase in the charges of free-quarter for the parliamentary army, so Winstanley's economic position deteriorated. Although he was able to maintain his residence and kept his friends and family, he felt this to be an experience of abject failure and loss. Parish church life was also unstable as the vicar left in 1644 and the parish was without a settled ministry until 1656. Winstanley read widely but found little comfort; he had a spiritual awakening through inner revelation during the winter of 1647-48 and stated that he had 'gone through the ordinance of dipping'. From 1648 Winstanley became the Digger's leader and spokesperson; most of his writings appeared between 1649 and 1652, when his last piece, *The Law of Freedom*, was published. The Diggers set up their community on St George's Hill but this collapsed in 1649; they moved to Cobham Heath and were dispersed in 1650. Winstanley returned to live in Cobham, where he had kept his residence and land. He became a waywarden of Cobham parish in 1659 and 1666, overseer of the poor in 1660, churchwarden in 1667 and 1668, and one of the two chief constables for the Elmbridge hundred in 1671. Legal documents for 1660-62 show him to have had the title of gentleman. By 1664 Winstanley's wife had died and her property was transferred from Winstanley to her sister. In 1664 he married Elizabeth Standley in St Giles Cripplegate. They had three children. In 1676, the burial register of the Westminster Quaker monthly meeting recorded the burial of Gerrard Winstanley, aged approximately sixty-two, corn-chandler of St Giles in the Fields.

George Fox

George Fox was born in Leicestershire in 1624. His father was a puritan weaver in good circumstances, and his mother was educated and 'of the stock of the martyrs'. His parents had originally intended George for the ministry of the Church of England but he was apprenticed to a shoemaker who was also a grazier and wool dealer. In 1643, Fox spent an evening at a fair drinking healths; he felt prompted to leave early and after spending a night in prayer he felt a divine call to forsake all existing associations. He turned south and moved between Lutterworth, Northampton and Newport Pagnell, avoiding religious and social contacts. In 1644, he moved to London, in a spiritual state verging on despair. Hearing that his family were concerned at his absence, he returned to Drayton. He spent about a year consulting clergy in an attempt to resolve his spiritual issues but in 1646 he gave up attendance at church, seeking God instead in the fields or orchards with his Bible. He wandered the midland counties mixing with various sorts of separatists and in 1647 'declared truth' at the independent church at Dukinfield. He went on to preach to Baptists and in Leicester in 1648 he spoke at a 'steeple-house' to a gathering of 'Presbyterians, independents, and common-prayer-men'. Shortly after this Fox received revelations about the functioning of nature; after considering whether to become a doctor, he decided that he would be more effective depending only on the light within rather than entering into formal systems of qualification. He engaged upon a course of aggressive action of preaching, teaching and healing, supported by sincerity in all personal interactions. His first incarceration was at Nottingham in 1649, for brawling in church. Fox's earliest recorded convert was a middle-aged widow in Nottingham, Elizabeth Hooton, who became the first woman preacher in the society. He soon had thousands of supporters, first known as 'Friends of the Truth;' in 1650 they were first called 'Quakers' as Fox had told the magistrates to 'tremble at the word of the Lord'. The Friends were organised as a network of groups; from 1652 this was assisted by Margaret Fell, the wife of Justice Fell, whose home in Lancashire became the headquarters of the movement, and to whom the travelling preachers sent their reports. An administrative system for the registration of births, marriages and burials began in 1652 and a system of targeted giving to help the poorest members was instituted. Fox made many missionary journeys across England and Wales and to Scotland, Ireland, the West Indies, North America and Holland. He was imprisoned eight times, the longest period being 1663-66; these periods enabled him to draw attention to appalling conditions. In addition to preaching, Fox produced a large number of publications, sometimes in conjunction with others. In 1669, he married Margaret Fell; she was ten years his senior and they had no children. Fox died in 1691 in London; four thousand people attended his burial.

Bibliography

Primary Sources

Argula von Grumbach, 'To the University of Ingolstadt', in *Radical Christian writings: a reader*, A. Bradstock and C Rowland, eds (Oxford, 2002)

Baxter, Richard, *The Reformed Pastor (1656),* W. Brown, ed. (Edinburgh, 1997)

The Bible, Authorized Version (London 1966)

The Bible - Latin Vulgate
<http://www.fourmilab.ch/etexts/www/Vulgate>
[accessed 28 January 2020]

The Book of Common Prayer
<http://justus.anglican.org/resources/bcp/1559/BCP_15 59.htm> [accessed 28 January 2020]

The Geneva Bible: a facsimile of the 1560 edition, Lloyd E. Perry, intro. (Massachusetts, 2007)

The Soldiers Pocket Bible 1643, Pryor Publications facsimile (Whitstable, 1997)

Bunyan, J., *Grace abounding to the chief of sinners* (Springdale, 1993)

Calvin, J., *Institutes of the Christian Religion*, J.T. McNeill, ed. and F.L. Battles, trans. (Philadelphia, 1960)

Fell, M., *Women's Speaking Justified* <http://www.qhpress.org/texts/fell.html> [accessed 28 January 2020]

Fox, G., *The journal of George Fox*, N. Penney, ed. (London, 1944)

Fox, G., *Book of miracles*, H.J. Cadbury, ed. (London, 2000)

Ignatius of Loyola, *The Spiritual Exercises*, Elder Mullan S.J., trans.<http://jesuit.org/jesuits/wp-content/uploads/The-Spiritual-Exercises-.pdf> [accessed 28 January 2020]

John of the Cross, *The complete works of St John of the Cross: Ascent of Mt Carmel, Dark night of the soul, Spiritual canticle, Poems, Living flame of love, Cautions and counsels, Spiritual sentences and maxims, Letters and documents*, E. Allison Peers, trans. and ed. (Wheathampstead, 1974)

Lefevre d'Etaples, Jacques, 'The restoration of the Gospel', in *The portable Renaissance reader*, J.B. Ross and M.M. McLoughlin, eds (Harmondsworth, 1954)

Morton, A.L., ed., *Freedom in Arms: a selection of Leveller writings* (London 1975)

Reuchlin, J., 'De verbo mirifico', Lyons, 1552, in *The occult philosophy of the Elizabethan Age*, F. Yates (London, 2002)

Teresa of Avila, *The complete works: vol. 2: Way of perfection, Interior castle, Conceptions of the love of God: vol. 3: Book of the foundations, Prose works, Methods for the visitation of convents of Discalced Carmelite nuns, Poems, Documents*, E. Allison Peers, trans. and ed. (London, 2002)

Teresa of Avila, *The life of Saint Teresa*, J.M. Cohen, trans. and ed. (Harmondsworth, 1958)

Teresa of Avila, *The Teresian Constitutions,* I. Moriones OCD, ed., and S.C. O'Mahoney OCD, trans. <http:/www.ocd.pcn.net/histo_4.htm> [accessed 28 January 2020]

Uitenhovius, J., 'John Uitenhovius to Henry Bullinger', in *Original letters relative to the English Reformation*, H. Robinson, ed. (Cambridge, 1847)

Ward, M., *The heart and mind of Mary Ward*, IBVM, ed. (Wheathampstead, 1985)

Ward, M., *Till God will: Mary Ward through her writings*, G. Orchard, IBVM, ed. (Slough, 1985)

Winstanley, G., *'The Law of Freedom' and other writings*, C. Hill, ed. (Cambridge, 1983)

Secondary sources

Allison Peers, E., *Spirit of Flame: a study of St John of the Cross* (London, 1943)

Alsop, J., 'Gerrard Winstanley: what do we know of his life?' in *Winstanley and the Diggers 1649-1999*, A. Bradstock, ed. (London, 2000)

Aylmer, G., 'The Diggers in their own time', in *Winstanley and the Diggers 1649-1999*, A. Bradstock, ed. (London, 2000)

Brenan, G., *St John of the Cross: his life and poetry* (Cambridge, 1995)

Byrne, L., *Mary Ward: A pilgrim finds her way* (Dublin, 1984)

Christian, W.A., *Local religion in sixteenth-century Spain* (Guildford, 1989)

Crawford, P., *Women and religion in England 1500-1720* (London 1996)

Davies, H., *Worship and theology in England from Andrewes to Baxter and Fox* 1603-1690 (Princeton, 1975)

Davis, J.C., 'Against formality: one aspect of the English Revolution', in *Transactions of the Royal Historical Society, 6th series, 3* (1993)

Davis, J.C., 'Cromwell's religion', in *Oliver Cromwell and the English Revolution*, J. Morrill, ed. (Harlow, 1990)

Discalced Carmelite Order, *St Teresa of Avila*, <http://www.ocd.pcn.net/teresa.htm>[accessed 20 March 2020]

Doran, S., and Durston, C., *Princes, Pastors and People: The Church and Religion in England 1529-1689* (London, 1991)

Durston, C., 'For the better humiliation of the people: public days of fasting and thanksgiving during the English Revolution', *The Seventeenth Century*, 7, (1992)

Evenett, H., *The spirit of the Counter-Reformation* (Cambridge, 1968)

Fenlon, D., *Heresy and obedience in Tridentine Italy: Cardinal Pole and the Counter Reformation* (Cambridge, 1972)

Friedman, J., *Miracles and the pulp press during the English Revolution* (London, 1993)

Hill, C., *The world turned upside-down* (London, 1991)

Hill, Clifford, *Prophecy past and present* (Guildford, 1995)

Hsia, R. Po-Chia, *The world of Catholic renewal 1540-1770* (Cambridge, 1998)

Kavanaugh, K., OCD, and Rodriguez, O., OCD, 'Biographical sketch', in *The collected works of St John of the Cross* (Washington, 1991)

Kendall, R.T., *Calvin and English Calvinism to 1649* (Oxford, 1979)

Kendall, R.T., *The way of wisdom: patience in waiting on God* (Carlisle, 2002)

Littlehales, M.M., *Mary Ward: pilgrim and mystic* (Tunbridge Wells, 1998)

Mack, P., *Visionary women: ecstatic prophecy in seventeenth-century England* (Berkeley and Los Angeles, 1994)

McGrath, A., *Christian theology: an introduction* (Oxford, 1994)

McGrath, A., *The intellectual origins of the European Reformation* (Oxford 1995)

McGregor, J.F. and Reay, B., eds, *Radical religion in the English Revolution* (Oxford, 1986)

Mills, M., *Human agents of cosmic power in Hellenistic Judaism and the Synoptic tradition* (Sheffield, 1990)

Moriones, I., OCD Teresa of Jesus, foundress of friars, S.C.Mahoney, trans. <http:/www. Ocd.pcn.net/histo_6.htm> [accessed 28 January 2020]

Mullett, M., *The Catholic Reformation* (London, 1999)

Munck, T., *Seventeenth-century Europe: state, conflict and the social order in Europe 1598-1700* (London, 1990)

Peters, H., *Mary Ward: a world in contemplation*, H. Butterworth, trans. (Leominster, 1994)

Stephen, L., and Lee, S., eds, *Dictionary of national biography, vol. VII* (Oxford, 1968)

Thomas, K., *Religion and the decline of magic* (London, 1991)

Tyacke, N., *Anti-Calvinists: the rise of English Arminianism* (Oxford, 1991)

Walter, J., 'The commons and their mental worlds', in *The Oxford history of Tudor and Stuart Britain*, J. Morrill, ed. (Oxford, 2000)

Wright, M., *Mary Ward's Institute: the struggle for identity* (Sydney 1997)

Yates, F., *The occult philosophy in the Elizabethan Age* (London, 2000)